A

POLITICAL

DICTIONARY

OF

BLACK QUOTATIONS

A
POLITICAL
DICTIONARY
OF
BLACK QUOTATIONS
REFLECTING
THE BLACK MAN'S
DREAMS, HOPES, VISIONS

SELECTED AND EDITED

BY

OSEI AMOAH

First published in 1989

Copyright © Osei Amoah

All rights reserved

BRITISH LIBRARY CATALOGUING IN PUBLICATION DATA

A Political Dictionary of Black Quotations:
Reflecting The Black Man's Dreams,Hopes, Visions.
1.Black Persons, Political Aspects.
I.AMOAH, OSEI
     305.8'96
            ISBN 0 9514035 0 8

Printed and published in Great Britain

SELECTED
BY
OSEI AMOAH

PUBLISHED BY OYOKOANYINAASE HOUSE,

UK: 23 Donnybrook Road, Streatham Vale,
London SW16 5AY
USA: 85 Sherman Street, Apt 103,
Pawtucket
Rhodes Island 02860

ACKNOWLEDGEMENT

A work of this magnitude is not possible without references to other works. Special thanks, therefore, are given to the authors and editors of the following publications:
Discourse on Colonialism, A Black Theology of Liberation, Malcolm X speaks, The Wretched of the Earth, Unity & Struggle, My People,My Vision, The Challenge of Nationhood, Profiles of African Leaders, Embattled Man, Towards Colonial Freedom, I speak of Freedom, Steve Biko, The Struggle is my Life, Africa must unite, I am prepared to die, W.E.B. speaks, The Struggle continues, The selected writings of W.E.B.Dubois, Marcus Gravey & the Vision of Africa, Neo Colonialism, The Black Viewpoints, The Sun will rise, Notes of a Native Son, Sixth Pan African Congress, Africa in World Politics, The Black Revolution, Black Leaders of the 20th Century, The new Creation, Black Power, Black Resistance to Apartheid, Ujama, Nnamdi Azikiwe Speeches.

DEDICATION

To all persons of whatever race and of whatever part of the world, who in various capacities and by their unremitting labours, have struggled through the years to liberate the black race so that the black generation could fight for reconstruction, The Editor dedicates this book with the ardent hope that before this century shall end, the black man, through his own manly efforts, aided by his friends, shall have reached that point in the world civilization, where he will be respected, recognised, and treated as any other World Citizen.

A NOTE TO THE READERS

Regretfully, this dictionary has not been as comprehensive or as representative of all the available disciplines as I would have wished. It is believed, however, that response will be spontaneous and more forthcoming after the emergence of this first edition.
Without claiming infallibility or inerrancy, it is hoped that this publication will be a welcome addition to your library.

In an effort to improve this dictionary, so that the user can be assured of its continuing usefulness, the Editor welcomes submissions of quotations, your comments and suggestions along with notes of omissions and, sources of quotations and short biographies of authors.
If you are seeking quotations to illustrate or develop or emphasize your speech or idea, you should turn to the table of themes and look for the appropiate subject heading. Or if you are looking for quotations by an individual author, you should turn to the index of authors which has page references. Some quotations appear under a number of themes.

An interesting feature of this book is that the arrangement of quotes under each theme forms a collective composition incorporating the sayings of a range of people. This is achieved by having the quotes on the theme compiled so as to present a flow of ideas.
To enable you to appreciate the quotations the

more, short biographical sketches of the authors have been included right at the end. You may choose to read them first before reading the quotations or vice versa.

CONTENTS

INTRODUCTION

The idea of compiling this volume stemmed from the following considerations:

a) To bring together within the covers of one book, in an easily accessible form, some of the well expressed thoughts, views, visions, hopes and aspirations of some of the most scholarly and prominent black spokesmen and women, past and present, on those matters appertaining to the BLACK MAN that are now preoccupying the attention of the civilised world.

b) To enlighten the black man on those vital topics relating to himself, and on those questions touching his development in civilization.

c) To indicate to black posterity the meaning of their forefathers' sacrifice, a sacrifice that will be a living and shining example to emulate.

d) To leave a legacy to posterity, a legacy that echos the burning desires of the black race.

The basis for inclusion of every quotation is the idea it encapsulates and the relevance of that idea to the black race. The selections included deal almost exclusively with the BlACK MAN of the past, of today, of the future, his aspirations, his frustrations, his victories, his defeats and his image of himself. Of course, there are differences in emphasis.

The spokesmen and women chosen are persons whose viewpoints are representative of a large number of persons. They are persons with national and international prominence among members of their race. In short, they are men and women with an audience and with a mechanism for disseminating their thoughts. Moreover they are men and women who have spoken out, who have addressed themselves to the economical, social, and political needs of the people at a crucial time.

Too often books seeking to represent viewpoints from various sources rely on personalities, stereotypical labels such as militant, moderate and conservative as a means of categorisation. Such approaches cloud basic issues and make it difficult for the reader to objectively appraise ideas and their significance. We have sought a more meaningful and pragmatic means of grouping men and ideas. The inclusion of black men and women of the nineteenth century, I feel, allows the reader to see a continuity of thought in the BLACK MOVEMENT through the years.

The passing of time will undoubtedly result in the emergence of new spokesmen and women, new statements. Consequently, some of those personalities identified here will be eliminated in one way or another while others will merely fade into obscurity. Yet their ideas and philosophies will remain, if not with active significance, certainly with historicity. Since this is true, the book empaphises thoughts and ideas for, ideas are more resistant to mortality than are men.

Now in sending forth this book, I, ardently hope and believe that it will not only accomplish the objects herein set forth, but that it will also do much towards bringing about a better and deeper understanding of the black man's problem, progress and destiny. Here is a book intensely interesting to all who are concerned about the continued advancement of the BLACK MAN.

Today, the BLACK MAN is gaining new faith in himself; he is beginning to "like" himself; he is discovering that the current theories and stories of "backward" peoples are largely lies and assumptions, that human genius and possibilities are not limited by colour, race or blood.

This book will do good. It is not a book that is read once and put away. It is a book to be returned to again and again. It serves a purpose not fulfilled or adequately represented by one person's speeches and writings. It must be stimulating to the black people. It must awaken in them self-respect, self-reliance and the ambition to be and to do. By the perusal of its pages they will be led to see more clearly and sensibly the weight of responsibilities resting upon them.

The BLACK MAN is realising the importance of self-help. This book will deepen that realisation, and ultimately lead him to imbibe in all its fullness the sentiment of the poet:

"DESTINY IS NOT ABOUT THEE BUT WITHIN;
THYSELF MUST MAKE THYSELF."

This amazing collection of views will offer a greater insight into himself and the world for which is being prepared. The reader will find himself confronted by the black man, speaking for himself, about himself, and for the good of his people.

As a whole, this book should be enjoyable and useful to a general audience as well as to a politically orientated audience, and in all cases where intellectual discourse is an essential part of the learning process.

Between these two covers lie the fruits of decades of research to be placed in the permanent collection of the library where present and future generations of the black race will find it a most significant document.

Osei Amoah
London, November 1988

THE PAST, THE PRESENT & THE FUTURE OF THE BLACK RACE

For nearly a generation we have been pushed along the wrong road. But now, in place of colonial detractors, is rising a new class of leaders, who with a wider horizon, a deeper sagacity and a true patriotism, are endeavouring to establish a foundation of morality, industry and knowledge and to build upon them a race that shall be capable of availing itself of every opportunity that the future may present, and worthy of whatever fortune it may bring.

DR. J.W.E. BOWEN

The great problem confronting this and future generations is and will be how to bring about results that make for the upbuilding of sterling character; how with the opportunity at our command to make the next fifty years of freedom and the entire future life proportionately worthy of honourable mention.

DR.J.W.E. BOWEN

In the horizon of Africa's future I see clearly the bright dawn of a Union Government, the birth of a great Nation which is no longer the dream of a new Utopia. Africa, the sleeping gaint,is now awake and is coming into her own.

KWAME NKRUMAH

The brighter day is rising upon Africa. Already I seem to see her chains dissolved, her desert plains red with harvest, her Abyssinia and Zululand the seats of science and religion, reflecting the glory of the rising sun from the spires of their churches and universities.

KWAME NKRUMAH

We want to create conditions such that in this generation disease, hunger, poverty, illeteracy and ignorance should begin to vanish for ever from our society.

SAMORA MOISES MACHEL

Steadily and firmly we are building up a better and richer life for our people and our continent.

The liberation flame, although feeble and glimmering, still grows brighter each day. And the time is approaching when a new civilisation, a new culture, shall spring up from among our people, and the Nile shall once again flow through the land of science, of art and of literature, wherein will live Black Men of the highest accomplishments.

KWAME NKRUMAH

The battle for humanity is not lost or losing. All across the skies sit signs of promise. The Slave is rising in his might, the yellow millions are tasting liberty, the black Africans are writhing toward the light, and everywhere the labourer, with ballot in his hand, is voting open the gates of opportunity and peace. We must not falter, we must not shrink. Above are the everlasting stars.

W.E.B. DUBOIS

The essence of development along your own lines is that you must have the right to develop and the right to determine how to develop.
It's essence is freedom and—beyond freedom— self-determination. This is the vision we hold for our future and our development.

CHIEF ALBERT LUTHULI

Today we have climbed the heights where we would open at least the outer courts of knowledge to all, display its treasures to many, and select the few to whom its mystery of truth is revealed, not wholly by birth or the accidents of the stock market, but at least in part according to deftness and aim, talent and character.

W.E.B. DUBOIS

A generation ago, the black man had practically nothing. He started out with scarcely a name - poor, degraded, demoralised, as slavery left him. Without a home, without a foot of land, without the true sense of real manhood, ragged, destitute, so freedom found him. From this humble beginning he has begun to acquire something of this world's goods. He has been getting for himself a home, some interests and he is bravely and consciously struggling toward the plane where his vindication as a man and a citizen is what he is and what he has acquired.

REV. M. MASON

Is the black man poor ? Yes, but he isn't always going to be poor. Ignorant ? Yes, but he isn't always going to be ignorant. The progress that he has already made in these directions shows clearly what the future is to be. Knowledge is power; wealth is power and that power the black man is getting.

F.J. GRIMBLE

8

A new civilisation, a new culture, shall spring up
from among our people, and the Nile shall once
again flow through the land of science of art and
of literature, wherein will live black men of the
highest learning and the highest accomplishment.

MARCUS GARVEY

The most difficult problem of our times is, how to
think, so that the black race may regain its lost
Paradise. We cannot apprehend and intelligently
grasp, the things that make for regeneration,
unless we think for ourselves fearlessly and even
aggresively. We must continue thinking-thinking of
the days that are no more, thinking of and for the
present, thinking of the unknown tommorow.

W.E.B. DUBOIS

The future of Africa lies within each and everyone
of us.
We are the future of Africa; every art of ours
whether good or bad, every deed, every word spoken
whether in jest or in truth will have some
significant effect upon the future of Africa.
Yesterday was Europe; from today it will be
Africa. Let the world see that the march is on,
let us win this battle not only for ourselves but
for our children's children and the future of
Africa.

DR. ABRAHAM JEROME

In the ancient times, Europe looked to Africa for new ideas for fresh inspirations, and the saying was perpetuated and handed down from generation generation ' Semper aliquid novi ex Africa ' - there is always something new from Africa.

> Now lies she there,
> And none so poor to do her reverence.

All because thinking in our age has become a lost Art.

REV.J.M. COX

Africa is no longer a thing apart, a continent of faceless millions. A vital force animates her being, and with the lifting of the white man's menace she seeks a place among the sons of the earth.

FRANK MARAES

In the early history of mankind, the black man stood high in the ladder of civilisation, but through the dark ages fell into ignorance and superstition; but now, in the yawning of a new day arising,never again to be submerged beneath the darkness that covers the earth and the gross darkness that covers the people.

REV. J.M. COX

The day has really arrived, when Africa begins her forward march and nothing will stop her, till she has reached the summit of glory and has been transformed into the great Africa we all dream of, for the future.

MARCUS GARVEY

Potentially, though, everything of importance in Africa has changed, and it has done so in a sense that may be called irreversible. It has changed so far that everything now seems possible where little or nothing seemed possible before.

BASIL DAVIDSON

Let us decide not to imitate Europe; let us combine our muscles and our brains in a new direction. Let us try to create the whole man, whom Europe has been incapable of bringing to triumphant birth.

FRANTZ FANON

Our people are moving together towards the achievement of a society where intellectual or functionary will no longer be dominant, a society in which we shall achieve more of the things which all people through all the time have acknowledged to be the legitimate goals of struggle: independence and equality.

W.E.B. DUBOIS

Africa must change; change from an area where people eke out an existence and adapt themselves to the environment,to a continent which challenges the enviroment and adapt to man's need.

JULIUS NYERERE

What is needed is a new society, a new pattern of daily life, a modern Africa equipped to join the modern world.

BASIL DAVIDSON

We live, work and pray for the establishment of a great and binding racial hierarchy, the founding of a racial empire whose only natural, spiritual and political limits shall be God and Africa, at home and abroad.

MARCUS GARVEY

I am becoming convinced day by day that the New Africa is destined to become a reality. No force under the heavens can stem it. Even my death cannot postpone its crystallisation.

NNAMDI AZIKIWE

Black consciousness is an attempt to recover a past deliberately destroyed by slave masters, an attempt to revive old survival symbols and create new ones.

J.H. CONE

For the African Dream is a tantalising dream that cannot be evaded, and it is up to us who live today to proclaim it everyday, everywhere, to fight for it and if necessary die for it, never allowing ourselves to carry the burden of insult and degradation or with falsehood and treacherous cunning try to build a shelter for our dishonoured manhood.

MOKWUGO OKOYE

Yesterday we were black and oppressed; today, our blackness is a tool for our liberation. Our dual status gives us a mythical right of citizenship and the concrete reality of our situation has given us the national consciousness of an oppressed and colonised people.

ELDRIDGE CLEAVER

It would be as well to decide at once to change our ways. We must shake off the heavy darkness in which we plunged, and leave it behind. The new day which is already at hand must find us firm, prudent and resolute.

FRANTZ FANON

13

Our society is being transformed into a new society in which man is in harmony with himself and with nature.

SAMORA MOISES MACHEL

We are men, human beings, capable of the same acts as any other race; possessing, under fair circumstances, the same intelligence as any other race. Africa has been sleeping for centuries – not dead, only sleeping. Today Africa is walking around, not only on its feet but on its brains.

MARCUS GARVEY

Africa demands a new look and an adapted structure. This can be done only in one way: by a healthy change of leadership and men.

LABERT U. EJIFOR

We are now face to face with a new order of things. Under this new regime we witness the foreshadowing of a higher sense of civilisation, a higher standard of morals, a broader field of culture and a purer realm of thought.

J.R. HAWKINS

Our dream is one of liberation, a right of self-determination, a dream of denied freedom, no more no less. Our fire says we are no longert dreaming of freedom, we are exercising our rights to be free at no expense of anybody who gets in our way.

H. RAP BROWN

Our desire is a place in the world. we must create a new Africa, a new Africa with a voice to speak, a new Africa with a voice to be heard, a new Africa to take her rightful place in the comity of nations. We believe that for our desire to come true the blood of Africa must flow.

MARCUS GARVEY

There is much to live for. I see before me a picture of a redeemed Africa, with her dotted cities, with her beautiful civilisation, with her millions of happy children going to and fro.

MARCUS GARVEY

The faith we have is a faith that will ultimately take us back to that ancient plane, that ancient position that we once occupied, when Ethiopia was in her glory.

MARCUS GARVEY

What our ancestors achieved gives us confidence that we can create out of that past, a glorious future, not in the terms of war and military pomp, but in terms of social progress and peace.

KWAME NKRUMAH

The future is neither wholly ours nor wholly not ours, so that we should not count upon it as quite certain or despair of it as quite not to come.

MOKWUGO OKOYE

The African of today is a modern man. He has a right to benefit by the development of technology and science. We need to conquer our deserts, tame our rivers, exploit our forest and prepare our youth for a new tomorrow.

TOM MBOYA

The faint and flickering light reveals how great the darkness has been. Some think that the shadows are lengthening into eternal night for the black man but that flickering light within has upon it the breath of God which will some day fan it into the white and penetrating blazer of the electro-carbon searchlight,that shall chase away the curse of slavery.

DR. J.W.E. BOWEN

The future may be a dream, but the present which
we possess is a reality.

MOKWUGO OKOYE

Africa of today presents a new fact to the
world,infused with new aspirations and aims, cal-
ling for recognition and a right to be admitted
into the community of nations of the world.

TOM MBOYA

We are creating a generation of black young people
who will know what they want, and they will create
a generation who will know how to get what they
want.

MALCOLM X

For ourselves and for humanity, we must turn over
a new leaf,we must work out new concept,and try to
set foot a new man.

FRANTZ FANON

In determining our future out of the lessons of
our present and past,we shall be working out a new
synthesis; a way of life that draws from Europe as
well as Africa,from Islam as well as Christianity,
from communualism and individualism.

JULIUS NYERERE

Through the children of today we believe we can build the foundation of the next generation upon such a rock of morality,intelligence and strength, that the floods of prejudice and injustice may descend upon it in torrents and yet it will not be moved.

MRS M.C. TERRELL

All of us may not live to see the higher accomplishment of an African empire, so strong and powerful, as to compel the respect of mankind, but we in our lifetime can so work and act as to make the dream a possibility within another generation.

MARCUS GARVEY

Our march to freedom has been long and difficult. There have been times of despair, when only the burning conviction of the rightness of our course has sustained us.Today,the tragedies and misunderstanding of the past are behind us.Today,we start on the great adventure of building a great nation.

JOM KENYATTA

For two hundred and fifty years we have been a race of slaves; for fifty years we have been a race of parasites. Now we propose to end all that. No more fear, no more cringing, no more sycopanthic begging and pleading !

MARCUS GARVEY

Africa needs a new type of citizen, a dedicated, modest, honest, informed man. A man who submerges self in service to the nation and mankind. A man who abhors greed and detests vanity. A new type of man whose humility is his strength and whose integrity is his greatness.

KWAME NKRUMAH

You cannot scare the negro any more. The negro is a man. His back is not yet to the wall; we do not want his back to the wall because that would be a peculiar position and desperate position. We do not want him there.

MARCUS GARVEY

The black man is fast learning that if he would be free,he, himself,must strike the blow. The heights are still beyond, but he is slowly rising, and day by day, hope grows brighter and brighter.

JULIUS NYERERE

The conditions under which we work and live are changing.Promising prospects are opening up before us. We are on the verge of a new nation; a new horizon opens before all of us as a people and we are determined never to fail.

JULIUS NYERERE

I can see springing up, cities of Africa becoming
the metropolis of science and learning archi-
tecture and philosophy. And the immortal are re-
sounding the echo: seek ye first the political
kingdom and all things shall be added unto you.

KWAME NKRUMAH

Africa must take initiative now. The tides are at
their fullest in Africa at the moment. Correspondingly, they are at their lowest in the
European World. As Africans, if we do not take the
opportunity now, nature and history will never
give us another chance.

DR. ABRAHAM JEROME

And so lifting as we climb, onward and upward we
go, struggling and striving and hoping that our
desires for total emancipation of the black man
will materialise before long. With courage, with a
keen sense of responsibility which we must
continue to assume, we look forward to the future,
large with promise and hope. seeking no favours
because of our colour or patronage, because of our
needs, we knock at the bar of justice and ask for
an equal chance.

MRS. ROSA D. BOWSER

Let us, then, wherever we are, resolutely struggle, in the believe that there is a better day coming, and that we,by patience,industry, uprightness, and economy may hasten that better day.

MARCUS GARVEY

We believe the time has come for us to strengthen the structures that we established so that we will be able to handle with greater determination and vigour the new challenging tasks which will arise in our efforts to achieve a revolutionary trans- formation of our society.

J.J. RAWLINGS

Today the whole country knows that their labours were not in vain, for a new spirit and new ideas have gripped our people. Today the people speak the language of action:there is a mighty awakening among the men and women of our country.

NELSON MANDELA

I am the equal of any white man. I want you to feel the same way. We have now come to the turning point of the Negro, where we have changed from the old cringing weakling, and transformed into full- grown men, demanding our position as MEN.

MARCUS GARVEY

The nations of the world are aware that the Negro of yesterday has disappeared from the scene of human activities and his place taken by a new Negro who stands erect, conscious of his manhood rights and fully determined to present them at all costs.

MARCUS GARVEY

The Uncle Tom nigger has got to go, and his place must be taken by the new leader of the Negro race. That man will not be a white man with a black heart, nor black man with a white heart, but a black man with a black heart.

MARCUS GARVEY

We do not want to go down in history as willing players in a game of charade over the future of our country.

TOM MBOYA

As Africans, we face grim imperatives. Africa is not a world unto itself but an integral part of one world. We have to make a new Africa in which all races of men live and work together in the great task of reconstruction.

WILLIAM TUBMAN

The way out is certainly not to regurgitate all Islamic or Euro-colonial influences in a futile attempt to recreate a past that cannot be resurrected. The way out is only forward, forward to higher and reconciled form of society, in which the quintessence of human purpose of traditional African society reasserts itself in a modern context - forward in short, to socialism, through policies that are scientifically devised and correctly applied.

KWAME NKRUMAH

Countrymen, we have committed ourselves to a revolutionary transformation of our society. That we shall never go back.
We must remind both our critics and admirers that revolution is not a one act play which happens once and it's all over.

J.J. RAWLINGS

We should go down to the grassroots of our culture, not to remain there, not to be isolated there, but to draw strength and substance therefrom, and with whatever additional sources of strength and material we acquire, proceed to set up a new form of society raised to the level of human progress.

SEKOU TOURE

Africa has first to repersonalise herself, move out from under the shadow of Europe and display her own virtues to her own delight, show the world that she too was an integral and inseparable part of humanity's achievement and endeavour.

BASIL DAVIDSON

Let us work to bring together the energy and intelligence of the entire people for peace, progress, prosperity and plenty. It is the task of us all to organise society so that we can conquer underdevelopment which is not our making.

SAMORA MOISES MACHEL

We aim to define and encourage a new consciousness among black people which will make it possible for us to proceed toward those answers and those solutions to our problems.

SKOLEY CARMICHAEL

We have to work hard to evolve new patterns, new social customs, new attitudes to life, so that while we seek the national, cultural and economic advancement of our country, while we raise our people's standard of life, we shall not sacrifice their fundamental happiness.

KWAME NKRUMAH

The launching of the struggle and the victories we have won reveal concretely that there is no such thing as fateful destiny;we are capable of transforming society and creating a new life.

SAMORA MOISES MACHEL

To have a flourishing economy is not enough, to have money and to create new enterprises is not enough. What is needed here is a profound awareness of the rights and responsibilities by whose sacred duty is to build a new society in which justice and equality would reign supreme.

RICAHRD ANDRIAMANJAJO

Today the people who yesterday could express no views on their lives and on their destiny, can express their view,can make decisions. This is a clear evidence that the struggle is of our people, by our people and for our people.

AMILCAR CABRAL

The black man of today is different from the black man of yesterday. He has shown to the world his aptitude for study and general improvement.By his industry he has made himself master of any situation into which he has been placed, and none will deny that his achievements along all lines have been commensurate with his opportunities.

JOSEPHINE S. YATES

We call upon you, Africans everywhere, whatever
your political attitudes, if you are feeling the
weight and consciousness - first of what Black
people are suffering, secondly, of what we have
achieved and are in the process of achieving, to
give the struggle your support so that before the
end of this century, perhaps we shall take a
leading part in the achievement of a society in
which we can look at our children, from the very
beginning of their lives, and know they are taking
a complete part in shaping the forces that touch
Africa and its people.

W.E.B. DUBOIS

Hitherto we have been viewed and have viewed
ourselves, as an impotent and spiritless race,
having only a mission of folly and degradation
before us. Today we stand at the portals of a new
world, a new life and a new destiny.

FREDERICK DOUGLAS

In this hour when the sun is just beginning to
climb the horizon of a new day in the life of the
black race, there is an imperative need for close
observation and serious, earnest thought. We cannot be content ourselves with appearances. We
cannot trust the decision reached mainly through
our emotioanl nature.

We must bring the whole personal conscious man into our meditation in order that we may see and comprehend that hand of God laid in love upon the black man of this continent.

PROF. JOSEPH D. BIBB

Civilised or not civilised, ignorant or illiterate, rich or poor,we , the African States, deserve a governement of our choice. Let us make our own mistakes, but let us take comfort in the knowledge that they are our own mistakes.

TOM MBOYA

I know we can reach our immediate goals, without a great deal of reflective thinking. But I doubt that we can build vitality for tomorrow without a lot of it for this is the way we get deeper understanding of our problems.

JULIUS NYERERE

The real thing in this world is not so much where we stand, as in what direction we are moving.

JULIUS NYERERE

HUMAN RIGHTS: THE BLACK RACE DEMAND

The black man has been actually worthless when it comes to exercising his rights as human beings in ever advancing civilisation. So we cannot demand recognition until we have some land that we can call our own.

ELIJAH MUHAMMAD

There will be neither rest nor tranquility in America until the Negro is granted his citizenship rights. The whirlwinds of revolt will continue to shake the foundations of our nation until the bright day of justice emerges.

MARTIN LUTHER KING, JNR

Freedom is the heritage of man and by freedom we do not mean freedom from the laws of nature, but freedom to think and believe, to express our thoughts and dreams, and to maintain our rights.

W.E.B. DUBOIS

In the present status of the black man it is particularly necessary that we today make the world realise what his position is, make them realise that he is not merely insisting on

Ornamental rights and neglecting plain duties, but
that the rights we want are the rights that are
necessary, inevitable before we can rightly do our
duties.

W.E.B. DUBOIS

The African demands the right to be a free citizen
in the South African democracy; the right to an
unhampered pursuit of his national destiny and the
freedom to make his legitimate contribution to
human advancement.

NELSON MANDELA

Freedom is as absolute as truth. You are either
lying or telling the truth. We were born free. We
must exercise our right to be free.

H. RAP BROWN

I believe in liberty for all men; the space to
stretch their arms and their souls, the right to
breathe and the right to vote, the freedom to
choose their friends, enjoy the sunshine, and ride
on the railroads, uncursed by colour; thinking,
dreaming, working as they will in a kingdom of
beauty and love.

W.E.B. DUBOIS

We will not be satisfied to take one jot or title less than our full manhood rights. We claim ourselves every single right that belongs to a freeborn American, political, civil, and social; and until we get these rights we will never cease to protest and assail the ears of America.

W.E.B. DUBOIS

We are men; we have souls, we have passions, we have feelings,we have hopes,we have desires,like any other race in the world. The cry is raised all over the world today of America for the Americans, of England for the English, of France for the French,of Germany for the Germans. Do you think it unreasonable that we, the blacks of the world, should raise the cry of Africa for the Africans.

MARCUS GARVEY

We do not desire to create offence on the part of other races; but we are determined that we shall be heard properly; that we shall be given the right to which we are entitled.

MARCUS GARVEY

In proportion as the race rises in intelligence and wealth, the valleys will be filled and the mountains will be levelled, that now stand in the way of his progress, in the way of the complete recognition of all of his rights.

F.J. GRIMBLE

Yet while we believe that Africa belongs to the Africans we are not racialists or chauvinists. We welcome into our midst peoples of all other races, other nations, other communities,who desire to live with us in peace and equality. But they must respect us and our rights, our right as the majority to rule. That, as our Western friends have taught us to understand it,is the essence of democracy.

KWAME NKRUMAH

Our dream is one of liberation, a right of self-determination, a dream of denied freedom; no more no less. Our fire says we are no longer dreaming of freedom, we are exercising our rights to be free at no expense of anybody who gets in our way.

H. RAP BROWN

The struggle of the black people is part of this universal struggle for equality and human dignity. We cannot survive a free nation if there is any part of the world in which people of Africa colour or descent are treated as subhumans. We seek to affirm our rights and place not just in Africa but in the bigger village called the world.

TOM MBOYA

Slavery and coloniasation has given the black man some of the arts of civilised life; but it must be added, that, denying him the inalienable rights of manhood, denying him the right to the product of his labour, it has left him no noble incentive to labour at these arts.

MRS. JOSEPHINE YATES

All of our people have the same goals, the same objective:freedom,justice, equality.All of us want recognition and respect as human beings. We are not fighting for integration, nor are we fighting for separation. We are fighting for the right to live as free humans. We are actually fighting for rights that are even greater than civil rights and that is human rights.

MALCOLM X

You may deprive a poor and ignorant people of their rights, and succeed in keeping them deprived of them,but you can't hope to do that when these conditions are changed;and the point to which I am directing attention here,is that this change is taking place.

F.J. GRIMBLE

We are asserting the right of Africa to determine its policies in its own interests, and to have an influence on world affairs which accords with the right of all people to live on this planet as human beings equal with other human beings. We are asserting the right of all people to freedom and self-determination; and therefore expressing an outright opposition to colonialism and international domination of one people by another.

JULIUS NYERERE

The essence of development along your own lines is that you must have the right to develop and the right to determine how to develop.
It's essence is freedom and- beyond freedom- self-determination. This is the vision we hold for our future and our development.

CHIEF ALBERT LUTHULI

In a world in which the oppressor defines right in terms of whiteness, humanity means an unqualified identification with blackness.

J.H. CONE

The people of Africa cannot continue to accept as their destiny the denial of human rights. We, too, have a right to live, to enjoy freedom, and to pursue happiness like other human beings.

NNAMDI AZIKIWE

Firmly and unfalteringly let the black race in
America,in Africa, in the West Indies and throughout the world close ranks and march steadily on,
determined as never before to work and save and
endure, but never to swerve from their great goal;
the right to stand as men among men throughout the
world.

W.E.B. DUBOIS

African freedom is not just an act of withdrawal,
but a major step in asserting the right and place
of the black people as equals among nations and
people of the world.

TOM MBOYA

Let us not try to be the best or worst of others,
but let us make the effort to be the best of our-
selves.The best in a race is not reflected through
or by the action of its copyists, but by its
ability to create of and by itself. It is such a
creation that the black man seeks.

MARCUS GARVEY

EQUALITY & JUSTICE FOR THE BLACK RACE

The time has come when one person ceases to employ another because he is of colour, but he employs the one who can give more than value received. The race needs to bring the hand and the head nearer together.

N. W. HARLLEE

The time is coming when racial prejudice shall have passed away, and when colour will no longer impede our obtaining what is due to us; then will justice and equity rule sublime, and the black man being protected in all his rights;his liberty, life and reputation will be held sacred, and virtue and worth will be considered;and man, the prince of God's creation will be crowned for doing justice unto man.

ISAAC PURCELL

The history of the American Negro is the history of this strife, this longing to attain self-conscious manhood, to emerge his double self into a better and truer self. In this merging he wishes neither of the older selves to be lost. He would not Africanise America, for America has too much to teach the world and Africa.

He would not bleach his Negro soul in a flood of white Americanism, for he knows that Negro blood has a message for the world. He simply wishes to make it possible for a man to be both a Negro and an American, without being cursed and spat upon by his fellows, without having the doors of opportunity closed roughly in his face.

TOM MBOYA

The history of the world, and of every nation is at bottom of man's struggle to reconcile the need for order in technologically changing society with his demand to associate as free individual on terms of equality with other men.

JULIUS NYERERE

We believe in the equality of races. We believe in the freedom of the people of all races. We believe in cooperation. In this struggle of ours, in this struggle to redeem Africa, we are fighting not against race and colour and creed. We are fighting against a system - a system which degrades and exploits.

KWAME NKRUMAH

Let the world take no backward step in that slow but sure progress which has successively refused to let the spirit of class, of privilige, or of birth, debar from life, liberty and pursuit of happiness a striving human soul.

W. E. B. DUBOIS

We are at war - all the black people - today. We would betray our own course if we were to desert, in any manner or form the battle for dignity, freedom and equal opportunity.

TOM MBOYA

And so lifting as we climb, onward we go, struggling and striving and hoping that our desires for total emancipation of the black man will materialise before long.
With courage, with a keen sense of responsibility which we must continue to assume we look forward to the future, large with promise and hope, seeking no favours because of our colour or patronage, because of our needs, we knock at the bar of justice and ask for an equal chance.

MRS. ROSA D. BOWSER

The African Revolution is not inspired by mere love of Revolution. It is inspired by the gross inequalities of our continent and our desire to eradicate these inequalities.

KWAME NKRUMAH

37

I believe in liberty for all men; the space to stretch their arms and their souls, the right to breathe and the right to vote, the freedom to choose their friends, enjoy the sunshine, and ride on the railroads, uncursed by colour; thinking, dreaming, working as they will in a kingdom of beauty and love.

W. E. B. DUBOIS

We are looking forward to a non-racial, just and egalitarian society in which, creed and race shall form no point of difference.

STEPHEN BIKO

The struggle of the black people is part of this universal struggle for equality and human dignity. We cannot survive a free nation if there is any part of the world in which people of Africa colour or descent are treated as subhumans. We speak to affirm our rights and place not just in Africa but in the bigger village called the world.

TOM MBOYA

A people's struggle is effectively theirs if the reason for that struggle is based on the aspirations, the dreams, the desire for justice and progress of the people themselves and not on the aspirations, dreams or ambitions of half a dozen persons who are in contradiction with the actual interests of their people.

AMILCAR CABRAL

I have a dream that one day this nation will rise up, live out the true meaning of its creed: we hold these truths to be selfevident that all men are created equal.

MARTIN LUTHER KING, JNR

We are citizens of one world, we are all of one blood. To hate a man because he was born in another country, because he speaks a different language, or because he takes a different view on this subject or that, is a great folly. Desist, I implore you, for we are all equally human... Let us have but on end in view, the welfare of humanity.

JOHN COMETRIUS

We are fighting a war today that individuals all over Africa may have freedom, equal chance for every man to have shelter or spell happiness to that particular human personality. If we believe firmly that peace cannot come to the world unless this is true for men all over the world, then we must know in our nation that every man, regardless of race and religion has this chance.

NNAMDI AZIKIWE

Our enemies, triumphant for the present are fighting the stars in their course. Justice and humanity must prevail.We live to tell these dark brothers of ours, scattered in counsel, wavering and weak - that no bribe of money or notoriety, no promise of wealth or fame, is worth the surrender of a people's manhood or the loss of a man's self-respect. We are men, we will be treated as men. On this rock we have planted our banners. We will never give up though the trump of doom find us still fighting.

W. E. B. DUBOIS

I believe in anything that is necessary to correct unjust conditions. I believe in it as long as it is intelligently directed and designed to get results. But I don't believe in getting involved in any kind of political action or other kind of action without getting down and analysing the possibilities of success or failure.

MALCOLM X

The black man's fight is a fight to the finish. Either he dies or wins. If he wins it will be by no subterfuge or evasion of amalgamation. He will enter modern civilisation as a black man on terms of perfect and unlimited equality with any white man, or he will enter not at all. Either extermination root and branch, or absolute equality. There can be no compromise.

FLOYD P. MCKISSICK

During my lifetime I have dedicated myself to this struggle of the African people. I have fought against white domination and black domination. I have cherished the ideal of a democratic and free society in which all persons live together in harmony and with equal opportunities. It is an ideal which I hope to live for and to see realised. If needs be, it is an ideal for which I am prepared to die.

WILTON NKWAYI

The American Negro demands equality - political equality, industrial equality and social equality;and he is never going to rest satisfied with anything less. He demands this in no spirit of braggadocio and with no obsequious envy of others, but as an absolute measure of self-defence and the only one that will assure to the darker races their ultimate survival on earth.

W. E. B. DUBOIS

Let every black American gird up his loins. We have crawled and pleaded for justice and we have been cheerfully spat upon and murdered and burned. We will not endure it forever. If we are to die, in God's name, let us perish like men and not like bales of hay.

W. E. B. DUBOIS

The twentieth century in its infancy is striving to grasp what it pleases to call the BLACK MAN's problem, when it is in reality only a question as to whether justice and right shall rule over injustice and wrong to any and every man regardless of race in this boasted land of freedom.

MRS. R. D. SPRAGUE

We want an Africa open to all, in which every kind of genius may grow.

FRANTZ FANON

The cost of liberty is less than the price of repression,even though that cost be blood. Freedom of development and equality of opportunity is our demand.

W.E.B. DUBOIS

Allow the black man two hundred and fifty years of unselfish contact to offset the two hundred and fifty years of cucasian selfishness, and be assidious in his regeneration as you were in his degradation - then judge him.

MRS.R.D. SPRAGUE

God grant that the refining fires of truth may burn until all the doors of prejudice shall be melted and consumed, when:

> " Man to man united
> The whole world shall be lighted
> As Eden was of old. "

MRS.M.E.C. SMITH

Nowhere are prejudices more mistaken for truth, passion for reason,and invective for documentation than politics.

J. MASON BROWN

While the cruelties of the white man toward the black man are among the heaviest counts in the indictment against humanity, colour prejudice is not our original fault, but only one aspect of the atrophy of the imagination that prevents us from seeing ourselves in every creature that breathes under the sun.

JAMES BALDWIN

If they really believe there is danger from the Negro it must be because they do not intend to give him justice.

BOOKER T. WASHINGTON

There is no more evil thing in this world than race prejudice. It justifies and holds together baseness, cruelty and, abomination than any other sort of error in the world.

H.G. WELLS

The equality of races, peoples or cultures has meaning only if we are talking about an equality in law, not an equality in fact.

AIME CESAIRE

If ever America undergoes great revolutions, there will be brought about the presence of black race in the soul of the United States, there will be their origin;not to the equality,but to inequality of condition.

ALEXIS DE TACQUEVILLE

If a man is my colour,and he is wrong,I am against him. If a man is my colour and he is right, I am for him. Let the Negro adopt this as a maxim and justice is his, and now and forever.

J. THOMAS HEWIN

The People of Africa cannot continue to accept as their destiny the denial of human rights. We, too, have a right to live, to enjoy freedom, and to pursue happiness like other human beings.

NNAMDI AZIKIWE

We are not fighting for the right to be like you. We respect ourselves too much for that. When we advocate freedom, we mean freedom for us to be black, or brown, and you to be white, and yet live together in a free and equal society. Our fight is not for racial sameness but for racial equality.

JOHN OLIVER KILLENS

Our tasks are clear...... We have to play our full part as world citizens in the development of humanity;to do that we have to shake off the mental effect upon ourselves of colonialism and discrimination. We have to fight colour prejudice and discrimination everywhere;and we have to assist, and where possible promote, the rights of all the world's citizens for an equal share of the world's resources.

JULIUS NYERERE

Whoever imposes oppression, however large or small the number of victims, and however understandable the feelings of fear or revenge which promote it racial discrimination is the mother of war, and suffering, and loss of freedom for everyone.For if men cannot live as men they will at least die as men.

JULIUS NYERERE

Man cannot drive fear into the heart of man, because man is but the equal of man. The world is crazy and foolish if they think that they can destroy the principles, the ideals of the Universal Negro Improvement Association.

JOHN HENRIK CLARKE

If and when we are all free and equal men, perhaps even those racial distinctions that now divide our societies and that separate our nation from the other will diaappear in the face of our common humanity.

TOM MBOYA

We believe that in our country there shall be no minority; just the people. And those people will have the same status before the law and the same political rights.

STEPHEN BIKO

We must destroy all ideologies that tend to divide us. All of us must register a new era of justice, equality, equal opportunity for everyone from every part of the world, regardless of creed, race and colour.

WILLIAM S. TUBMAN

The Black Man is ignored today simply because he has kept himself to a higher state in the civilised cosmos, all the other races would be glad to meet him on the plane of equality and comradeship. It is indeed unfair to demand equality when one of himself has done nothing to establish the right to equality.

JOHN HENRIK CLARKE

Steadfastness, therefore, in the faith that moves mountains and patience which overcomes a world of wrong and injustice, will bring the reward as it has so often done with the race in the past. The reward is perfect equality. But our attitude must be one of absolute fidelity to the priceless sacred trust of citizenship, which comes to us out of the agonies of the greatest war of modern times.

T.T. FORTUNE

Before this century shall have ended, the black man through his own manly efforts, aided by his friends, shall reach that point in the world of civilisation, where he will be recognised and treated as any other world citizen.

DR. D.W. GULP

Only when we are granted independence will the struggle stop. Only when our human dignity is restored to us, as equals of the whites, will peace be between us.

ELISER TUHADELEEN

The prejudices of the whites against the blacks have rather helped him in that they have stimulated him to make greater efforts to reach the independence of the white man. What seems a curse is in reality a blessing to the race.

PROF W.H. COUNCILL

There will be neither rest nor tranquility in America until the Negro is granted his citizenship rights. The whirlwinds of revolt will continue to shake the foundations of our nation until the bright day of justice emerges.

MARTIN LUTHER KING, JNR

We feel that the world as a whole has a special responsibility towards us. This is because the land of our forefathers was handed over to South Africa by a world today. It is a divided world, but it is a matter of hope for us that it at least agrees about one thing - that we are entitled to freedom and justice.

HERMAN JA TOIVO

We are asserting the right of Africa to determine
its policies in its own interests, and to have an
influence on world affairs which accords with the
right of all people to live on this planet as
human beings equal with other human beings. We are
asserting the right of all peoples to freedom and
self-determination; and therefore expressing an
outright opposition to colonialism and international domination of one people by another.

JULIUS NYERERE

We are men; we will be treated as men. We will
never give up, though the trump of doom find us
still fighting.And we shall win. The past promised
it, the present foretells it.

W.E.B. DUBOIS

Our people are moving together towards the
achievement of a society where intellectual or
functionary will no longer be dominant, a society
in which we shall achieve more of the things which
all people through all the time have acknowledged
to be the legitimate goals of struggle: independence and equality.

W.E.B. DUBOIS

Today, in spite of our military coups and cesspools of corruption and conflicting tribulations, our darkness recedes and in the lightening landscape we begin to see our people more clearly - a kindly and smiling people even under the burden of injustice and misfortune.

MOKWUGO OKOYE

As long as Africa lives her people are bound to be obsessed by the urge for freedom and unity and equality which she has inspired, and someday they will be able to translate this instinctive urge into a pulsating reality.

MOKWUGO OKOYE

To have a flourishing economy is not enough, to have money and to create new enterprises is not enough. What is needed here is a profound awareness of the rights and responsibilities by whose sacred duty is to build a new society in which justice and equality would reign supreme.

RICHARD ANDRIAMANTATO

As a race we must strive by race organisation, by race solidarity, by race unity to the realisation of that broader humanity which freely recognises differences in men, but sternly depreciates inequality in their opportunities.

W.E.B. DUBOIS

50

If you cannot live alongside the while man in peace, if you cannot get the same chance and opportunity alongside the white man, even though we are his fellow citizen;if he claims that you are not entitled to this chance or opportunity because the country is his by force of numbers then find a country of your own and rise to the highest position within that country.

MARCUS GARVEY

The problem of the twentieth century is the problem of the colour line, the question as to how far differences of race - which show themselves chiefly in the colour of the skin and the texture of the hair - will hereafter be made the basis of denying to one half of the world the right of sharing to their utmost ability the opportunities and privileges of modern civilisation.

W. E. B. DUBOIS

The world still belongs to the nationalists. We, who incorrectly regard ourselves as beyond or in some sense too old for nationalism, cannot deny it to others by pretending it is always outmoded or dangerous. Every person needs the consciousness that he is part of an efficacious order, and that when it is threatened, men will come to lead, inspire, to articulate what must be done to preserve it or establish a new order.

JULIUS NYERERE

Even though we face the difficulties of today and yesterday, I have a dream that one day my children will live in a nation where they will not be judged by their colour of their skin, but by the content of their character.

MARTIN LUTHER KING, JNR

If the great battle of human right against colour prejudice is to be won, it must be won not in our day, but in the day of our children's children. Ours is the blood and dust of battle, theirs is the rewards of victory.

W.E.B. DUBOIS

One fact is fundamental to the future of this continent, and of the world. Humanity is indivisible. No man can live with self-respect, or deserve the respect of others, if he acquiesces in the humiliation of human beings on the ground of colour or race.

JULIUS NYERERE

MASTERS OF OUR AFFAIRS, DESTINY & DECISIONS

The struggle in our land must be made by our people. We cannot for a moment think of liberating our land of building, peace and progress in our land, by bringing foreigners from outside to come and struggle for us.

AMILCAR CABRAL

Our time will come, and when it comes as dawn follows dusk, we shall reserve to ourselves the right to pick and choose our friends.

NNAMDI AZIKIWE

We are determined to maintain our mastery over our own destiny-to defend our national freedom. We are determined to change the condition of our lives. It is to meet these two needs that we must have both change and stability.These two must be inter-related for neither is possible without the other.

JULIUS NYERERE

We are now owners of our countries and societies. Let us work together to face new problems in such a way as to transform our heritage into an imperisable legacy.

NNAMDI AZIKIWE

Let us not deceive ourselves at our situation in this country. Weighted with a heritage or moral iniquity from our past history, hard pressed in the economic world by foreign immigrants and native prejudice, hated here, despised there and pitied everywhere our one haven of refuge is ourselves, and but one means of advance, our own belief in our great destiny, our own implicit trust in our ability and worth.

W.E.B. DUBOIS

The African people cannot be read out of history. Not to know what one's race has done in former times, is to continue always as a child. The African himself, expresses the thought in saying "knowing thyself better than he who speaks of thee. Not to know is bad; not to wish to know, is worse".

JULIUS NYERERE

The stakes are really very simple: if we fail to do this, we face continued subjection to a white society that has no intention of giving up willingly or easily its position of priority and authority. If we succeed, we will exercise control over our lives, politically, economically and psychologically.

STOKELY CARMICHAEL

We do not expect that independence will end our troubles, but we do believe that our people are entitled-as are all peoples-to rule themselves. It is not really a question of whether South Africa treats us well or badly, but that South West Africa is our country and we wish to be our own masters.

HERMAN JA TOIVO

The individual, the race, the nation, that helps itself is helped by God. The individual, the race or nation that leaves its destiny to forces completely exterior is doomed, and in the destruction there is no remorse, there is no shedding of tears by anyone but the sufferer himself.

MARCUS GARVEY

It is the black man's will to be free that has made him fight for this country. The army is to kill people. We have to decide if we will be killers; when we decide, we have to decide who we are going to kill, and when. We must be masters of our own decisions.

H. RAP BROWN

Today we are standing at the crossroads - one leads to wealth and power, the other to destruction. We have to decide which road we must follow.

MARCUS GARVEY

For the black people to adopt their methods of relieving our oppression is ludicrous. We blacks must respond in our own way, on our own terms, in a manner which fits our temperament. The definitions of ourselves, the roles we pursue, the goals we seek are our responsiblity.

STOKELY CARMICHAEL

Africa desires to be understood and to be recognised from the viewpoint and perspective of her own people. She cannot be a projection of Europe nor any longer permit herself to be interpreted or spoken for by self-appointed interpreters.

TOM MBOYA

Our destiny is in our own hands. It is beginning to dawn on us generally, that if we would be saved, we must save ourselves. We have it to do or reap the very bitter consequences. We have the ability and capacity to reach the highest point, and even to go further in the march of progress than has been made by any people.

GEORGE L. KNOX

We have no designs to elbow out of South Africa anyone, but equally we have no intention whatsoever of abandoning our divine right, of ourselves determining our destiny according to the holy and perfect plan of our creator.

CHIEF ALBERT LUTHULI

All problems in a nation's life must be unravelled and solved by that nation. It may take advantage of foreign influences and examples, incorporate and utilise them but the real work must be done by the nation itself.

PROF. J.D. BIBB

We Africans, in order to assert and maintain our rank as men, must speak for ourselves. No outside tongue, however, gifted with eloquence can tell our story. No outside eye, however penetrating, can see our wants. No outside Organisation, however benevolently intended, nor however cunningly contrived, can develop the energies and aspirations which make up our mission.

JULIUS NYERERE

We are fighting in order that in Africa there may exist a government chosen by the people, representing the will of the people and working for the good of the people of Africa. We fight so that we may destroy colonialism in every one of its forms.

EQUINO DE BRAGANCA

Civilised or not civilised, ignorant or illiterate, rich or poor, we, the African States, deserve a government of our own choice. Let us make our own mistakes, but let us take comfort in the knowledge that they are our own mistakes.

TOM MBOYA

What is wanted now is action. Let us all, through our concerted action build upon the solid foundations laid for us by the illustrious fathers of Pan Africanism, strive to build for ourselves and our future progeny,the better world that our oppressors have completely failed even to conceive. We have a duty to perform. Let us each go home and do it. We are our own liberators. Let us be free tomorrow, alive or even dead.

JUMBA ABBOUD

We have the right to govern and even to misgovern ourselves.

KWAME NKRUMAH

Africa must take initiative now. The tides are at their fullest in Africa at the moment. Correspondingly,they are at their lowest in the European World.As Africans, if we do not take the opportunity now, nature and history will never give us another chance.

DR. ABRAHAM JEROME

To allow a foreign country, especially, one which is loaded with economic interests in our continent, to tell us what political decisions to take, what political courses to follow, is indeed for us to hand back our independence to the oppressor on a silver platter.

KWAME NKRUMAH

58

Our surge to revolutionary reforms is late. If it is so - if we are late in joining the modern age of social enlightment, late on gaining self-rule, independence and democracy, it is because in the past the pace has not been set by us.

CHIEF ALBERT LUTHULI

We are aware that the white man is sitting at our table.We know he has no right to be there; we want to remove him.... strip the table of all trappings put on by him, decorate it in true African style, settle down and then ask him to join us on our own terms if he wishes.

STEPHEN BIKO

This has become a continent in the full ferment of deciding, of trying to decide, of believing that it can decide and thinking that it must decide, its course into the different years ahead.

BASIL DAVIDSON

At every stage of development people must know what their basic needs are. and just as they will produce their own food if they have land, so, if they have sufficient freedom they can be relied upon to determine their own priorities.

JULIUS NYERERE

'... If Africa has to be redeemed, if Africa has to make her own contribution to the world, if Africa is to take her rightful place amomg the continents, we shall have to proceed on different lines and evolve a policy which will not force her institutions into an alien European mould, but which will preserve her unity with her own past, conserve what is precious in her past, and build her future progress and civilisation on specifically African foundations. That should be the new policy, and such a policy would be in line with the traditions of the British Empire...'

KWAME NKRUMAH

FREEDOM AND INDEPENDENCE OF THE BLACK RACE

If self-government is a leprosy, I should be the first to be attacked.

KWAME NKRUMAH

A man is either free or he is not. There cannot be any apprenticeship for freedom.

LEROI JAMES

Freedom that is merely a slogan is the most decep-tive of slaveries;thus the black community chooses to be free in fact.

REV. JESSE JACKSON

Seek ye first the political kingdom and all other things shall be added unto it.

KWAME NKRUMAH

People cannot be denied liberty. For man is so conditioned that he will not rest unless he feels that he has freedom and human dignity which goes with it.
He will sooner or later, by one means or another, fight for his own freedom within society, and for the freedom of his society.

JULIUS NYERERE

You can't seperate peace from freedom because no
one can be at peace unless he has freedom.

MALCOLM X

Freedom is essential to development. But freedom
does not mean, and must not be allowed to mean,
the freedom of the rich and the 'clever' to
exploit the poor and ignorant.

JULIUS NYERERE

There is no easy walk to freedom anywhere and many
of us will have to pass through the valley of the
shadow of death and again before we reach the
mountain tops of our desires.

NELSON MANDELA

We have long suffered and today we want to breathe
the air of freedom. The Creator has given us this
share of the earth that goes by the name of the
African Continent;it belongs to us and we are it's
only master.
It is right to make this continent a continent of
justice, law and peace.

PATRICK LUMUMBA

It is in the nature of man to yearn and struggle for freedom. The germ of freedom is in every individual, in anyone who is a human being. In fact, the history of mankind is the history of man struggling and striving for freedom.

CHIEF ALBERT LUTHULI

And so for us Black Power heralds the long-awaited day of liberation from the shadows of obscurity. We take our place among the people of the world without hate or apologies, with confidence and with goodwill towards all men. The spectre of Black Power has taken shape and form and its material presence fights to end the exploitation of man by man.

KWAME NKRUMAH

The cost of liberty is less than the price of repression even though that cost be blood. Freedom of development and equality of opportunity is our demand.

W.E.B. DUBOIS

Freedom is within our grasp. Let us no longer quake or doubt about our capacity to enter into rightful heritage. Let there be no mistake about our future. We are determined to discard the yoke of oppression. We shall be free. History is on our side.

NNAMDI AZIKIWE

Our march to freedom has been long and difficult. There have been times of despair, when only the burning conviction of the rightness of our course has sustained us.Today,the tragedies and misunderstanding of the past are behind us. Today, we start on the great adventure of building a great nation.

JOMO KENYATTA

To be free is to participate in a community of those who are victims of oppression. Man is free when he belongs to a free community seeking to emancipate itself from oppression.

J.H. CONE

A people who free themselves from foreign domination will not be culturally free unless, without underestimating the importance of positive contributions from the oppressors's culture and other cultures, they return to the upwards paths of their own culture.

AMILCAR CABRAL

So long as we are undaunted and determined to be a free people, the fire of freedom shall not be extinguished from our hearths, we shall march forward towards our national emancipation.

NNAMDI AZIKIWE

Man, once awakened to the truth that freedom from oppression and freedom to engage in productive creativity are within his grasp, will never remain content to be a slave.

HUEY P. NEWTON

From our knowledge of the history of man, from our knowledge of colonial liberation movements, freedom or self-government has never been handed over to any colonial country on a silver platter.

KWAME NKRUMAH

I believe that there is a destiny for the black people of Africa and that such destiny can only be realised succesfully under the aegis of free and independent African Nations.

NNAMDI AZIKIWE

The African demands the right to be a free citizen in the South African democracy; the right to an unhampered pursuit of his national destiny and the freedom to make his legitimate contribution to human advancement.

NELSON MANDELA

Let us march together to freedom saying: The road to Freedom may be long and thorny but because our cause is just, the glorious end- Freedom - is ours.

CHIEF ALBERT LUTHULI

We prefer self-government with danger to servitude in tranquility.

KWAME NKRUMAH

The liberty of a country, like that of an individual must be limited to the extent that it must not make a nuisance of itself to other countries.

SIR ALIHAJI ABUBAKAR BALEWA

Freedom and development are as completely linked together as are chickens and eggs.Without chickens you get no eggs; and without eggs you soon have no chickens.
Similarly, without freedom you get no development, and without development you very soon lose your freedom.

JULIUS NYERERE

Freedom involves the full realisation of our identities and potential. It is in this sense that the objective of the African must be the development of his nation and the preservation of his heritage.

TOM MBOYA

If and when we are all free and equal men, perhaps even those racial distinctions that now divide our societies and that separate one nation from the other will disappear in the face of our common humanity.

TOM MBOYA

Your homes are under puppet regimes teleguided by neocolonialism. Real black freedom will only come when Africa is politically united. It is only then that the black man will be free to breathe the air of freedom, which is his to breathe, in any part of the world.

KWAME NKRUMAH

Freedom is as absolute as truth. You are either lying or telling the truth. We were born free. We must exercise our right to be free.

H. RAP BROWN

The people of Africa cannot continue to accept as their destiny the denial of human rights. We, too, have a right to live,to enjoy freedom and to pursue happiness like other human beings.

NNAMDI AZIKIWE

Freedom for black people is not an act of withdrawal, but a major step in asserting the rights of black people and their place as equals among nations and peoples of the world.

TOM MBOYA

If there is the possiblity of achieving political independence, man must defy all economical , social, cultural and geographical stabilities.

KWAME NKRUMAH

Freedom, or independence, is not an end in itself. It cannot mean merely political sovereignity with a national flag.

Independence is for us the means by which to ensure self-expression in social, cultural as well as economic fields.

TOM MBOYA

The profoundest commitment possible to a dark creator in this country today - beyond all creeds, craft, classes, and ideologies whatsoever - is to bring before his people the scent of freedom.

OSSIE DAVIS

Freedom is the heritage of man and by freedom we do not mean freedom from the laws of nature, but freedom to think and believe, to express our thoughts and dreams, and to maintain our rights.

W.E.B. DUBOIS

Destiny has now thrown the spotlight on Africa. It is now with the light of joyous and determined peoples, rushing to obtain political goals. Behind the shouting and dancing had long lurked a great determination to be free.

THOMAS P. MALADY

Freedom always entails danger. Complete Freedom never exits. But of all freedom of which we think, the freedom to learn is in the long run the least and the one that should be curtailed last.

W.E.B. DUBOIS

The African fought for freedom and independence for Africa. An African slave is just bad if not worst than a European slaver. We want neither of these conditions on the Continent of Africa. What the people want is national,political and economic freedom. Nothing short of freedom in a cultural plan will suffice.

DR ABRAHAM JEROME

The future beckons at us to dare the monsters that menace us. We are no fools for entering the social struggle even though we perish, for wise men still believe that it is better to be maimed or killed in their affray than to live like a slave.

MOWUGO OKOYE

We feel that the world as a whole has a special responsibility towards us. This is because the land of our forefathers was handed over to South Africa by a world body. It is a divided world, but it is a matter of hope for us that it at least agrees about one thing, that we are entitled to freedom and justice.

HERMAN JA TOIVO

The liberation of Africa is the task of Africans. We Africans alone can emancipate ourselves.We welcome the expressions of support from others, for it is good to know that we are wished well in our struggle;but we alone can grapple with the monster of Imperialism which has all but devoured us.

KWAME NKRUMAH

Africa wants her freedom, Africa must be free. It is a simple call,but it is also a signal lighting, a red warning to those who would tend to ignore it.

KWAME NKRUMAH

The wind of change and freedom has begun to rise and the Savannah under its breath shivers with a new hope.

MARCUS GARVEY

If we are to live our lives in peace, in harmony and without interference, if we are to change and improve the conditions under which we live, we must have at all costs total emancipation. For emancipation means freedom,freedom from exploitation,freedom from humiliation,freedom to determine our destiny, freedom from which will flow the results of our struggle, freedom to control and use the fruits of our resources.

JULIUS NYERERE

Let freedom ring from every hill. When we allow freedom to ring from every town and every hamlet, from every state and every city, we will be able to speed up that day when all God's children, black and white men will be able to join hands, and sing, "Free at last! free at last! Great God Almighty we are free at last!".

MARTIN LUTHER KING, JNR

Now is the time; the hour, the 'magna hora' of our emancipation has struck and the consolidated unity of all sane black men is needed to rally round the pivot on top of which is kindled the light, the light of our liberty.

MARCUS GARVEY

Although the flames Nkrumah lit may flicker in the years immedediately ahead, if only because great men like him are not born every day, the light of Nkrumah will some day, somehow, roar into an illumination.For he is not dead but lives in the hearts of freedom -loving peoples everywhere - a legend of faith and herois in the face of great odds.

MOKWUGO OKOYE

If life is to be complete, it must included not only the dimension of length but also of breath by which the individual concerns himself in the welfare of others.

MARTIN LUTHER KING, JNR

Africa was once great when it was free and it can and will be great again when it is free. But it cannot be great again until it is free.

MARCUS GARVEY

I know no national boundary where the Negro is concerned. The whole world is my province until Africa is free.

MARCUS GARVEY

We demand for Black Africa autonomy and independence, so far and no further than it is possible in this one world for groups and peoples to rule themselves, subject to inevitable world unity and federation.

JULIUS NYERERE

Our demand for self-government is a just demand. It is a demand admitting of no compromise. The right of a people to govern themselves is a fundamental principle, and to compromise on this principle is to betray it.

KWAME NKRUMAH

I am happy, and shall remain so, as long as you keep the flag flying.If I die in Atlanta, look for me in the whirlwind or the storm, look for me all around you, for with God's grace I shall come and bring with me the countless millions of black slaves who have died in America and West Indies and the millions in Africa to aid you in the fight for liberty, freedom and life.

MARCUS GARVEY

To allow a foreign country, especially, one which is loaded with economic interests in our Continent, to tell us what political decisions to take, what political courses to follow, is indeed for us to hand back our independence to the oppressor on a silver platter.

KWAME NKRUMAH

We face an enemy that is deep-rooted, an enemy entrenched and determined not to yield. Our march to freedom is long and difficult. But both within and beyond our borders, the prospects of victory grow bright.

DR ALEX EKWUEME

At every stage of development people must know what their basic needs are. And just as they will produce their own food if they have land, so, if they have sufficient freedom they can be relied upon to determine their own priorities.

JULIUS NYERERE

Such a change is within our power. It does not demand an economic strength which we do not have, it requires only a political consciousness, and a political will. And these depend upon our courage and intensity of our desire for real independence.

JULIUS NYERERE

As long as I enjoy the confidence of my people, and as long as there is a spark of life and energy in me,I shall fight with courage and determination for the freedom of all Africans irrespective of colour or creed.

WALTER SISULU

Christian theology is a theology of liberation.

N J.H. CONE

The economical development of Africa demands, indeed, that Africa must first of all be free, absolutely free to think, free to carry out her creative activities, free in her relationship with nature, free in her economic, political and military relations , and free to assert her presence in the world as a factor contributing to the wealth of mankind.

SEKOI TOURE

The struggle for African freedom may be long and gloomy, but out of the cloud of suffering and disappointment loom the rays of hope and success on the distant horizon.

NNAMDI AZIKIWE

In these days of struggle for racial survival, let us not be bitter; let us bear no malice; let us be charitable and stand firm in the cause of justice and righteousness. God knows we hate none on account of race or colour, but we love our continent, and we want our countries to be free, and we shall be free.

NNAMDI AZIKIWE

We Africans, however, equally understand that much as others might do for us, our freedom cannot come to us as a gift from abroad. Our freedom must make ourselves. What we need is the courage that rises with danger.

CHIEF ALBERT LUTHULI

It is inevitable that in working for Freedom some of us must take the lead and suffer. The road to Freedom is via the cross.

CHIEF ALBERT LUTHULI

As long as Africa lives her people are bound to be obsessed by the urge for freedom and unity and equality which she has inspired, and someday they will be able to translate this instinctive urge unto a pulsating reality.

MOKWUGO OKOYE

It is only in conditions of total freedom and independence from foreign rule and interference that the aspirations of our people will see real fulfilment and the African genius find its best expression.

JULIUS NYERERE

We have taken the correct road, even though
hazardous. We face death as we face life with head
up, eyes lifted, proud and unafraid. The seed dies
that life may love forth. So we may meet death
knowing that we cannot be defeated. For the
oppressed people of the world will one day
triumph.

KWAME NKRUMAH

For us, for our people and for our land, the time
has come to put an end to indecisions and promises, to adopt definite action. We have already
made too many sacrifices, but we are determined to
make more to recover our freedom and human dignity, whatever the path to be followed.

AMILCAR CABRAL

What is important for our situation is that we are
all here. That we cannot change ! ...and since we
are all here we must seek a way whereby we can
realize freedom. More and more people are coming
to accept that and to work for it.

CHIEF ALBERT LUTHULI

The time has passed when they could rule the country as if we, the people, did not exist. The time is against them, the world is against them. We on the other hand are encouraged by the great spirit of the people of South Africa, by the growth of the national liberatory movement, by the unprecedented political consciousness of the people and by the fact that the truth is with us. We enjoy the confidence of the whole world in this noble and just task for which we are pledged to fight until the dawn of freedom.

WALTER SISULU

Man's greatest possession is life, declared Lenin, and since it is given to him to live but once, he must so live as not to be smeared with the shame of a cowardly existence and trivial past, so live that, dying, he might say: all my life and all my strength were given to the finest cause in the world - the liberation of mankind.

MOKWUGO OKOYE

What is wanted now is action. Let us all, through our concerted action build upon the solid foundations laid for us by the illustrious fathers of Pan Africanism, strive to build for ourselves and our future progeny, the better world that our oppressors have completely failed even to conceive.
We have a duty to perform. Let us each go home and do it.We are our own liberators.Let us be free tomorrow, alive or even dead.

JUMBA ABBOUD

The struggle for the total liberation of Africa is a struggle for human dignity and freedom. It is a struggle for peace, security, democracy and progress.

HASHIM MBITA

The way of preparation for action lies in our rooting out all impurity and indiscipline from our organization and making it the bright and shining instrunment that will cleave its way to Africa's freedom.

NELSON MANDELA

We have passed through more trials than most European countries and I believe we have come to appreciate freedom to a point where we would be prepared to defend it with our lives. We do not intend to exchange British Colonialism for either local dictatorship or Soviet and American economic colonialism.

TOM MBOYA

The developing countries face the challenge of development.There is no alternative but to prosecute the task of development with resolution in the knowledge that independence would be reduced to a mere slogan if this challenge is not met boldly.

TOM MBOYA

It is becoming more and more clear to us that to win our freedom is only the first hurdle in a long march. There are still many difficulties ahead. The struggle will be longer, the work greater and more difficult. By uniting the entire people in a common effort, with indomitable will and in a planned way, we shall succeed.

PROF. JOSEPH BIBB

The black man is fast learning that if he would be free, he, himself, must strike the blow. The heights are still beyond, but he is slowly rising, and day by day, hope grows brighter and brighter.

JULIUS NYERERE

We are about to enter a new phase. All of us Africans want to make this decade a decisive one. In fact, it is our determination to fight, leaving no stone unturned, sparing no life or blood when it is called for, to see Africa free and independent. This is our solemn commitment; this is our solemn resolve.

SAM NUJOMA

We need to remind ourselves that yesterday belonged to our fathers, but today is ours, as tommorow belongs to posterity.The younger generation is determined to usher in a new era of freedom and socialism before Time has broken the backs of its members.

MOKWUGO OKOYE

As long as we are ruled by others we shall lay our mistakes at their door and our sense of responsibility will remain dulled.Freedom brings responsibility, and our experience can be enriched only by the acceptance of these responsibilities.

KWAME NKRUMAH

This is our country. We are under a stern inescapable obligation to our consciences, to our people, and to God, to live and be with our people in these trying times and for better and for worse until victory is won and liberty and people and prosperity are restored and established in our land.

WILLIAM OFORI ATTA

Our war is not against Hitler in Europe, but against Hitler in America. Our war is not to defend democracy, but to get a democracy we have never had.

HARVARD STIKOFF

We see the day when Africa will be free and free forever. We have declared to the whole world that the African race must be emancipated from the industrial and educational boundage.

MARCUS GARVEY

The black people have freed themselves from the dead weight of the albatross of blackness that once hung about their neck. They have done it by picking it up in their arms and holding it out with pride for all the world to see.They have done it by embracing it, not in the dark of the moon but in the searing light of the white sun. They have said "Yes" to it and found that the skin that was once seen as symbolising their shame is in reality their badge of honour.

SHIRLEY CHISHOLM

We as a people have a great future before us. Let us work and wait patiently. For our day of racial triumph will come. Let us not divide ourselves into castes, but let us all work together for the common good.

MARCUS GARVEY

I know no national boundary where the Negro is concerned. the whole world is my province until Africa is free.

MARCUS GARVEY

Political independence is a fact for large areas of Africa and Carribean. Colonialism has begun its journey out of life and into the museums of history. We now have to recognise that an end to colonialism is not an end to oppression based solely on colour.

JULIUS NYERERE

The white man need expect no more Negro blood shed on his behalf. The first dying that is to be done by the black man in the future will be to make himself free.

MARCUS GARVEY

We are fighting a war today so that individuals all over Africa may have freedom, equal chance for every man to have shelter as spell happiness to that particular human personality. If we believe firmly that peace cannot come to the world unless this is true for men all over the world, then we must know in our nation that every man, regardless of race and religion, has this chance.

NNAMDI AZIKIWE

The Freedom we demand is for our country as a whole; this freedom we are claiming is for our children for generations yet unborn, that may see the light of day and live as men and women with the right to work out the destiny of their own countries.

KWAME NKRUMAH

It is our duty to hold aloft the torch of democracy so that our posterity shall be free. It is an obligation for us to prevent repetition of the fatal mistake of living in servitude and in want in the midst of plenty.

NNAMDI AZIKIWE

The liberation of women is not an act of charity. It is not the result of a humanitarian or compassionate postion. It is a fundamental necessity for the Revolution, a guarantee of its continuity, and a condition for its success.

SAMORA MOISES MICHEL

Only Africa free to develop its vast potential without hampering restrictions by the old colonial Powers could properly advance the interests of its several parts.Only Africa with centralised political direction could succesfully give effective material and moral support to Africans not yet free.

BASIL DAVIDSON

So the struggle continues and our national independence must not be seen as an end in itself but a means to the total liberation, unification and social transformation of Africa.

MOKWUGO OKOYE

We believe that the blood of Africa must flow to free Africa. Africa is the last continent the black man has to fight for and if he gives up fighting that will be the end of him.

JULIUS NYERERE

History is our inspiration, and our reward is the joy of serving the highest cause in the world, the liberation of mankind.

MOKWUGO OKOYE

As Africans, we must exercise the freedom of choice. The choice is between African life and European death. A choice between Africa and Europe. The conditions are clear cut as this. We can no longer sacrifice ourselves for a bit of crumbs off the masters's table. We have to build our own table. Not only that, we have to make and bake our own bread. Moreover, the bread must be African. Neither are we going to buy or borrow the flour,the wheat will be planted on African soil by African hands.

DR. ABRAHAM JEROME

Up you Mighty Race. You can accomplish what you
will. It is only a question of a few years when
Africa will be completely colonised by black race
as Europe is by the white race. No one knows when
the hour of Africa's redemption cometh. It is in
the wind. It is coming. One day, like a storm, it
will be here.

MARCUS GARVEY

African Unity is a political kingdom which can
only be gained by political means. Except by our
united efforts will the richest and still enslaved
parts of our continent be free from colonial
occupation and become available to us for the
total development of our continent, to create our
own progress and make our valuable contribution to
world peace.

KWAME NKRUMAH

We want peace, freedom and cooperation between men
and between all peoples. But for this very reason
and cause, we must put an end to colonialism in
our land, we must remove all obstacles to our
national independence, we are fighting and are
going to eliminate all those who, with weapons in
hand, seek but certainly in vain to prevent the
liberation of our people.

AMILCAR CABRAL

Our dream is one of liberation, a right of self-
determination, a dream of denied freedom; no more
no less. Our fire says we are no longer dreaming
of freedom, we are exercising our right to be free
at no expense of anybody who gets in our way.

H. RAP BROWN

We prefer poverty in liberty to wealth in slavery
and we will not renounce and will never renounce
our legitimate and natural rights to independence.

SEKOU TOURE

Merely by describing yourself as black you have
started on a road towards emancipation, you have
commited yourself to fight against all forces that
seek to use your blackness as a stamp that marks
you but as a subservient human being.

STEPHEN BIKO

Let us truly pledge to work together in love of
Freedom for all in our lifetime, not just freedom
for Europeans only, and as we march, pledge to
struggle together for freedom.

CHIEF ALBERT LUTHULI

With independence a new phase in struggle for
nationhood begins. For those who seek fulfilment,
the challenge of development offers the most
exiting and rewarding experience. The search for
unity must continue. The urgent needs of the
people cannot wait, for there is no probationary
period for a newly independent state.

TOM MBOYA

With one mind, one will, and one heart, we will
soon make Africa, our Africa, a really free and
independent continent.

PATRICK LUMUMBA

No black man, let him be American, West Indian or
African, shall be truly respected until the race
as a whole has emanicipated itself, through self-
achievement and progress from universal prejudice.

MARCUS GARVEY

We are not fighting for the right to be like you.
We respect ourselves too much for that. When we
advocate freedom, we mean freedom for us to be
black, or brown, and you white, and yet live together in a free and equal society. Our fight is
not for racial sameness but for racial equality.

JOHN OLIVER KILLENS

Unity and struggle mean that for struggle unity is necessary but to have unity it is also necessary to struggle. Unity for us to struggle against the colonialists and struggle for us to achieve our unity, for us to construct our land as it should be.

AMILCAR CABRAL

We must form a united front against the exploitation of man by man;we must cure ourselves of our complexes by a supranational awareness, a national consciousness. Our ridiculous divisions are profitable only to the great powers, which exploit our weaknesses.

LEON MBA

There is no time to waste for we must unite now or perish since no single African State is large or powerful enough to stand on its own.

KWAME NKRUMAH

Today we are one. If in the past colonialism didvided us, now it unites us and the sufferings of one are the sufferings of all.Divided we fall; united we could make Africa once more the seat of greatness. From this conference must go a new message: " Hands off Africa !" We must show the world that we are in earnest ! We must show ourselves as part of that world, the whole world, with a United Africa playing its special part in world affairs.

KWAME NKRUMAH

Let us from henceforth recognize one and all of the race as brothers and sisters of one fold. Let us move together for the one common good, so that those who have been our friends and protectors in the past might see the good that there is in us.

JOHN HENRIK CLARKE

Stand together in this new world and let the old world perish in its greed or be born again in new hope and promise.

W.E.B. DUBOIS

Our task at this moment must be one of collective effort. Success must be nationally gained and nationally felt. Africa's success is not something to be considered individually. The intellectuals must lead the masses. Let us rediscover ourselves. Let us rediscover Africa. Let us commit ourselves fully to the future development of Africa. Let us destroy imperialism. Let us bring to light the New Age.

DR. ABRAHAM JEROME

With one mind, one will, and one heart, we will soon make Africa, our Africa, a really free and independent continent.

PATRICK LUMUMBA

If Africa unites, it will be because each part, each nation, each tribe gives up a part of his heritage for the good of the whole. That is what union means;that is what Pan-Africa means.

W.E.B. DUBOIS

Africa Unity is a potential kingdom which can only be gained by political means. Except by our united efforts will the richest and still ensalved parts of our continent be free from colonial occupation and become available to us for the total development of our continent, to create our own progress and make our valuable contribution to world power.

KWAME NKRUMAH

Let us decide not to imitate Europe; let us combine our muscles and our brains in a new direction. Let us try to create the whole man, whom Europe has been incapable of bringing to triumphant birth.

FRANTZ FANON

There is nothing which unites a people as strongly as a common enemy. What we need is a common enemy. The point, however, is that we have such an enemy, not in another planet but here on Earth, namely the poverty of the so-called developing nations.

TOM MBOYA

We all want a United Africa, united in our common desire to move forward together in dealing with all problems that can best be solved only on continental basis.

KWAME NKRUMAH

Only when the black people fully develop the sense of community, of themselves, can they begin to deal effectively with the problems of racism in this country. This is what we mean by a new consciousness; this is the first vital step.

STOKELY CARMICHAEL

One nation is one ideal, one destiny is one secular faith in a better tomorrow for all Africans.

ARTHUR NNWANKO

Africa must unite. Africa must be strong, Africa must be respected. Africa must play its part in world affairs. A united Africa is bound to become the greatest nation the world has ever seen.

KWAME NKRUMAH

We have a common enemy. We have this in common: we have a common oppressor, a common exploiter, and a common discriminator. But once we all believe that we have a common enemy, then we unite on the basis of what we have in common.

MALCOLM X

The glory which awaits Africa cannot come about until Africa is united. If we fail to unite then a great nation will go to sleep forever.

KWAME NKRUMAH

The high tide of political and economic transformation in the African Continent, the high tide of the unification of our people, the high tide of cooperation among the people, has already swept the whole Continent - these are the basic assurances of victory of our cause.

KWAME NKRUMAH

It is a matter affecting our security. It is central to everything we try to do. It is not that we are great altruists who love freedom so much that we will fight for it everywhere and anywhere. We know our limitations. We know that people can only free themselves and no one can do it for them. We are all Africans; we all need to work together for the real development of any of us.

JULIUS NYERERE

Let us truly pledge to work together in love of Freedom for all in our lifetime - not just freedom for "Europeans only", and as we march pledge to struggle together for freedom.

CHIEF ALBERT LUTHULI

We cannot confront the European Culture with gunpower, and win. Our only hope is for us to use our African Culture and thought power to unite ourselves and overwhelm the European culture.

BARBARA MAKEDA LEE

We as a people have a great future before us. Let us work and wait patiently. For our day of racial triumph will come. Let us not divide ourselves into castes, but let us all work together for the common good.

MARCUS GARVEY

I appeal to you as a race to cultivate race pride, not race prejudice. Stand up like men and women and cultivate unity and protect and defend each others's interest. Let the elevation of one be the joy of the other, instead of pulling down those who are trying to elevate themselves and the race. If there are men among us who can be the means of bringing better conditions to the great black masses, and who can weed out the slow, dull, plodding process of evolution, they should not be denied the opportunity.

GEORGE L. KNOW

With independence a new phase in the struggle for nationhood begins. For those who seek fulfilment, the challenge of development offers the most exiting and rewarding experience. the search for unity must continue. The urgent needs of the people cannot wait, for there is no probationary period for a newly independent state.

TOM MBOYA

We have to create our own wealth, and we can only do this if we work together using at the begining simply the resources we already have - that is, our labour, our land, and our willingness to work together.

JULIUS NYERERE

What is wanted now is action. Let us all, through our concerted action build upon the solid foundations laid for us by the illustrious fathers of Pan Africanism, strive to build for ourselves and our future progeny, the better world that our oppressors have completely failed even to conceive. We have a duty to perform. Let us each go home and do it. We are our own liberator. Let us be free tomorrow, alive or even dead.

JUMBA ABBOUD

We can no longer come to terms with a situation where throughout the world all races should be free except the black race;where everything white is good and everything black is bad; where everything white is civilised and everything black is uncivilised. And that is precisely what the struggle is about, and that is why we must unite to change this state of affairs.

SEKOU MOBUTU

We must destroy all ideologies that tend to divide us. All of us must register a new era of justice, equality, equal opportunity for everyone from every part of the world,regardless of creed, race and colour.

WILLIAM S. TUBMAN

We have the capability to help each other in many ways, each gaining in the process. And as a combined people we can meet the wealthy nations on every different terms, for though they may not need any one of us for their own economic health, they cannot cut themselves off from all of us.

JULIUS NYERERE

We must recognise and fight the external and internal enemy and combine all our resources in the great struggle which lies ahead. With cohesive planning and with a full awareness of our united strength, nothing can halt the progress towards final victory.

KWAME NKRUMAH

The forces that unite us are greater than those that divide us, and our goal must be Africa's dignity, progress and prosperity.If we can achieve this example of a continent knit together in common policy and purpose, we shall have made the finest possible contribution to world peace.

KWAME NKRUMAH

While we are engaged in building the unity and greatness of Africa, we are aware of the fact that to be able to bring our aspirations to fruition, no aspect of our life should be interfered with in the name of continental interests. The African people will never harbour any foreign interference which may occur in various guises. Not at any stage can our efforts be thwarted, and we warn those who try to do so, that we will react to prevent it.

KWAME NKRUMAH

Firmly and unfalteringly let the black race in America, in Africa, in the West Indies and throughout the world close ranks and march steadily on, determined as never before to work and save and endure, but never to swerve from their great goal; the right to stand as determent menamong men throughout the world.

W.E.B. DUBOIS

Freedom, unity and cooperation should be the noble objectives of all peoples. But these will never be assured if we fail to create the right conditions which all Africans, despite varying customs,traditions and culture,can wholeheartedly support.

WILLIAM S. TUBMAN

There is a battle to be fought, there are obstacles to be overcome. There is a world struggle for human dignity to be won. Let us address ourselves to the supreme tasks that be ahead. To accomplish these aims, AFRICA MUST UNITE.

KWAME NKRUMAH

The decision has been made, the decision to fight for our freedom. Together we fight. It's your fight, it's my fight, it's our fight, it's the people's fight. If we cannot live as free people then we will fight dying as people.

MARCUS GARVEY

The time for drawing up plans is now past. Africa today must act. The peoples of Africa are waiting impatiently for such action to begin. Africa Unity and Solidarity are no longer mere dreams; we must now embody them in concrete decisions.

PATRICK LUMUMBA

We found we were unanimous as we fought our first battles against colonialism. We found we were unanimous as we mourned our dead brothers. We found we were unanimous at the Round Table, united in a Common Front. Today, in victory, in triumph, we are still united and unanimous: our entire nation rejoices at this.

PATRICK LUMUMBA

Suspicion and distrust of those who do not always think identically with us will not help the revolutionary process. All those whose goal is to secure a just society should be limited by that goal, and not divided by bickering over the exact path to take.

J.J. RAWLINGS

We are now owners of our countries and societies. Let us work together to face new problems in such a way as to transform our heritage into an imperishable legacy.

NNAMDI AZIKIWE

As a race we must strive by race organisation, by race solidarity, by race unity to the realisation of that broader humanity which freely recognises differences in men, but sternly depreciates inequality in their opportunities.

W.E.B. DUBOIS

We cannot allow ourselves to be disorganised and divided. To us. Africa is just one Africa, one and indivisible. We need to unify our efforts, our resources, our skills and intentions. The unity and strength of the unions of America States or Soviet Republics, should be our example.

KWAME NKRUMAH

We are oppressed because we are black. We must use that very concept to unite ourselves and respond as a cohesive group.

STEPHEN BIKO

Your homes are under puppet regimes teleguided by neocolonialism, real black freedom will only come when Africa is politically united. It is only then that the black man will be free to breathe the air of freedom, which is his to breathe,in any part of the world.

KWAME NKRUMAH

Africa is no longer a thing apart,a continent of faceless millions. A vital force animates her being, and with the lifting of the white man's menace she seeks a place among the sons of earth.

FRANK MARAES

It is becoming more and more clear to us that to win our freedom is only the first hurdle in a long march. There are still many difficulties ahead. The struggle will be longer, the work greater and more difficult. By uniting the entire people in a common effort, with indomitable will and in a planned way, we shall succeed.

PROF. JOSEPH BIBB

Now is the time; the hour, the 'magna hora' of our emancipation has struck and the consolidated unity of all sane black men is needed to rally round the pivot on top of which is kindled the light, the light of our liberty.

MARCUS GARVEY

Under a major political union of Africa, there could emerge a great and powerful nation in which the territorial boundaries which are relics of colonialism will become obsolete and superfluous.

KWAME NKRUMAH

Our cultural identity and common historical destiny should be our main concern as we have all been treated unjustly by exploiting powers. We should be able to identify ourselves, not by the colour of our skin, which is a static element, but solely in terms of our goals which are just and noble.

SEKOU TOURE

Let freedom ring from every hill. When we allow freedom to ring from every town and every hamlet, from every state and every city, we will be able to speed up that day when all God's children, black and white men will be able to join hands, and sing, "Free at last! free at last! Great God Almighty we are free at last!

MARTIN LUTHER KING.JNR

I will say to all Africans that if we must have justice, we must come together; if we must come together, we can only do so through the system of oraginisation. Let us not waste time in breathless appeals to the strong while we are weak, but lend our time, energy and effort to the accumulation of strength among ourselves by which we will attract the attention of others.

KWAME NKRUMAH

All Africa has one single aim; our goal is a united Africa in which standards of life and liberty are constantly expanding; in which the ancient legacy of illiteracy and disease is swept aside; in which the dignity of man is rescued from beneath the heels of colonialism.

CHIEF ALBERT LUTHULI

It is only through unity that our people can bargain, it is only through unity that they can discuss matters between themselves and settle their differences. In this way they can negotiate on an equal basis with other nations. Only in this way can they hope to develop.

KWAME NKRUMAH

As long as black people anywhere continue to be oppressed on the grounds of their colour, black people everywhere will stand together, in the future as in the past.

JULIUS NYERERE

In this advanced age, if the black man would scale the delectable heights already attained by more highly favoured races, we must unite in our endeavours to uplift our race. With unity of action and persistent struggle, all things are possible. Gather them,your forces; elevate yourself to some lofty height where you can behold the needs of your race; leave no stone unturned in your endeavour to rout the forces of all opposition; and ere long Africa's sons and daughters will be elevated among the enlightened races of the world.

MRS BISHOP C. PETTEY

Africa's hour has really arrived. Let us take steps to unite and protect our dear continent. If we stand firmly by our decisions, it is unlikely that we shall be disappointed. We are all pillars of the new Africa. Any weakness on our part means the everlasting collapse of Africa. Let us implore Providence to inspire us so that we may never lose sight of the true cause, and we may deserve the honour of sharing the future with Africa.

MARCUS GARVEY

I have a dream that one day the sons and daughters of former slaves will be able to get together at the table of brotherhood, ...that one day a state sweltering with the heat of injustice, sweltering with the heat of oppression, will be transformed into an oasis of freedom and justice.

MARTIN LUTHER KING, JNR.

You don't fight racism with racism. The best way to fight racism is with solidarity.

BOBBY SEALE

Black people must redefine themselves, and only they can do that. Throughout this country, vast segments of the black communities are beginning to recognise the need to assert their own definitions to reclaim their history, their culture; to create their own sense of community and togetherness.

STOKELY CARMICHAEL

Let us work to bring together the energy and intelligence of the entire people for peace, progress, prosperity and plenty. It is the task of us all to organise society so that we can conquer underdevelopment which is not own making.

SAMORA MOISES MACHEL

Africa in world politics appears in a new light of dignity, considerable experience and solidality: a bloc to be recognised,a group to be reckoned with, knit together in cooperation and mutual supplementation. Africa will no longer be the Dark Continent. It will remain the Black Continent but with its own formidable attribute - Black Power.

LAMBERT EJIOFOR

We are looking forward to a non-racial, just and egalitarian society in which colour,creed and race shall form no point of difference.

STEPHEN BIKO

The 1950's presided over the struggle for political emancipation. But the 1960's, whatever trials they have brought, have not been wasted. They have successfully opened the way for another necessary struggle,a struggle for the fruits of political emancipation, for that new and unified society without which the peoples of Africa cannot even keep the freedom which they have,let alone enlarge it.

BASIL DAVIDSON

As long a Africa lives her people are bound to be obsessed by the urge for freedom and unity and equality which she has inspired, and someday they will be able to translate this instinctive urge into a pulsating reality.

MOKWUGO OKOYE

Now it is for the white races to come together and give us a United States of Black Africa. If they want the Artic ocean, they can keep the Artic Ocean. If they want the moon, we are reasonable enough even to say,'Have it !' But we are going to have our part of Africa whether they will or not. We are going to have it.

MARCUS GARVEY

THE BLACK MAN'S STRUGGLE

If there is no struggle, there is no progress. Those who profess to favour freedom yet depreciate agitation, are men who want crops without ploughing up the ground;they want rain without thunder and lighting. They want the ocean without the awful roar of its many waters.

FREDERICK DOUGLAS

The history of the human race has been a struggle for the removal of mental, moral and spiritual oppression, and we would have failed had we not made our contribution to the struggle.

ROBERT SOBUKWE

The struggle, in the face of obstacles and in a variety of forms, reflects the awareness or grasp of a complete identity, generalises and consolidates the sense of dignity, strengthened by the development of political conciousness, and derives from the culture or cultures of the masses in revolt one of its principal strengths.

AMILCAR CABRAL

There come in all political struggles rare moments hard to distinguish but fatal to let slip, when caution is dangerous. Then all must be on a hazard, and out of the simple man is ordained strength.

KWAME NKRUMAH

We are men; we will be treated as men. We will never give up, though the trump of doom find us still fighting. And we shall win. The past promised it, the present foretells it.

W.E.B. DUBOIS

The battle which is to decide the future role of blacks has begun. The struggle will be long and hard. All black men, educated and uneducated, sick and well, weak and strong, young and old must stand and fight. If we fail, at this decisive moment, then our fate will be sealed forever.

MARCUS GARVEY

We are fighting and fighting desperately for the right to work and to get from our work food, housing, education, health and a chance to live as human beings. But in this fight we are not alone. With us stand and must stand whether they will or not, the white worker of America and of the World.

W.E.B. DUBOIS

We shall have to struggle for the right to create our own terms through which to define ourselves and our relationship to the society, and to have these terms recognised. This is the first necessity of a free people, and the first right that any oppressor must suspend.

STOKELY CARMICHAEL

The African in every part of this vast Continent has been awakened and the struggle for freedom will go on. It is our duty to offer what assistance we can to those now engaged in the battle which we ourselves have fought and won. Our task is not done, and our safety not assured until the last vestiges of colonialism have been swept from Africa.

KWAME NKRUMAH

We should wage the struggle by associating ourselves with the great struggle of all people in order to live a full and responsible life in a world of harmony, progress, peace, and justice. Since we are among the people who are oppressed most throughout history, we should raise our struggle to world-wide level and make our liberation the decisive element of the struggle of all people.

SEKOU TOURE

The only time we have is now. So now we must demand the impossible. Now we must struggle for the impossible. Now we must live for the imposible. Now we must die for the impossible. Only then will it burst into the realm of the possible. Only then will our bright and morning star replace the rocket's red glare. Only then will our sons and daughters be free.

VINCENT HARDING

Our people cannot expect progress as a gift from anyone, be it the United Nations or South Africa. Progress is something we shall have to struggle and work for. And I believe that the only way in which we shall be able and fit to secure that progress is to learn from our experience and mistakes.

HERMAN JA TOIVA

There is a battle to be fought, there are obstacles to be overcome. There is a world struggle for human dignity to be won. Let us address ourselves to the supreme tasks that lie ahead. To accomplish these aims, AFRICA MUST UNITE.

KWAME NKRUMAH

Unity and struggle mean that for struggle unity is necessary, but to have unity it is also necessary to struggle. Unity for us to struggle against the colonialists and struggle for us to achieve our unity for us to construct our land as it should be.

AMILCAR CABRAL

Our struggle - our resistance - must be waged on all levels of the life of our people. We must destroy everything the enemy can use to continue their domination over our people, but at the same time we must be able to construct everything that is needed to create a new life in our land.

AMILCAR CABRAL

But the struggle for African dignity, personal and national worth, the struggle for progress and improving the quality of life will not have come to an end. It will continue. The evil spirit in man that led to slavery, colonialism, capitalism, and racism will not have been exorcised.

HERBERT CHITAGO

Let us, then, wherever we are, resolutely struggle, in the believe that there is a better day coming, and that we, by patience, industry, uprightness and economy may hasten that better day.

MARCUS GARVEY

The struggle is a truly national one. It is a struggle of the African people, inspired by their own suffering and their own experience. It is a struggle for the right to live.

NELSON MANDELA

Our struggle against South Africa is an unequal one. But David slew Goliath because he had right on his side, and we Namibians have faith that we, too, have right on our side.

ELIASER TUHADELEEN

We are about to enter a new phase. All of us Africans want to make this decade a decisive one. In fact, it is our determination to fight, leaving no stone unturned, sparing no life or blood when it is called for, to see Africa free and independent. This is our solemn commitment; this is our solemn resolve.

SAM NUJOMA

The very bitterness of current controveries is itself an indication of our progress. For the struggle has been joined; the victims no longer acquiesce in their own degradation and many people are no longer willing to be identified with the humiliation of other men just because their colour is different.

JULIUS NYERERE

The close links forged between Africans and peoples of African descent over half a century of common struggle continue to inspire and strengthen us. For, although the outward forms of our struggle may change, it remains in essence the same, a fight to death against oppression, racism and exploitation.

KWAME NKRUMAH

The true nature of the struggle taking place in Africa and the world between the forces of progress and those of reaction is in the final analysis the fight of the common man against injustices and privileges.

KWAME NKRUMAH

We are going to begin another struggle, my brothers, my sisters, a sublime struggle that will bring our country peace, prosperity and grandeur.

PATRICK LUMUMBA

We call upon you, Africans everywhere, whatever your political attitudes, if you are feeling the weight and consciousness, first of what Black People are suffering, secondly, by what we have achieved and are in the process of achieving, to give the struggle your support so that before the end of this century, perhaps we shall take a leading part in the achieving of a society in which we can look at our children from the very beginnings of their lives, and know they are taking a complete part in shaping the forces that touch Africa and its people.

W.E.B. DUBOIS

The 1950's presided over the struggle for political emancipation. But the 1960's, whatever trials they have brought, have not been wasted. They have succesfully opened the way for another necessary struggle, a struggle for the fruits of political emancipation, for that new and unified society without which the peoples of Africa cannot even keep the freedom which they have, let alone enlarge it.

BASIL DAVIDSON

The history of the American Negro is the history of this strife,this longing to attain self-consciousness manhood, to merge his double self into a better and true self... He would not Africanise America, for America has too much to teach the world and Africa. He would not bleach the Negro soul in a flood of white Americanism, for he knows that the Negro blood has a message for the world. He simply wishes to make it possible for a man to be both a Negro and an American without being cursed and spat upon.

JAMES L. FARMER

Life for us in the conflict ahead is all stern and serious. Wounds and scars will for generations yet to come be the decorations for our leaders in thought and action.

PROF T. DE TUCKER

Let us reinforce our rank and file in the fight for freedom, no longer suffering in silence and whinning like a helpless dog, but striking back with all the force at our command when we are struck, preferring to suffer the consequences of pressing forward our claim to a legacy of freedom, than to surrender our legacy to despoilers and usurpers.

NNAMDI AZIKIWE

The road is long and full of difficulties. At times the route strays off course, and it is necessary to retreat; at times a too rapid pace seperates us from the masses, and on occasions the pace is slow and we feel upon our necks the breath of those who follow upon our heels.

NNAMDI AZIKIWE

Our duty is to wage our struggle in our land. Neither in Africa, nor anywhere else are we going to wage the struggle for others. We are to struggle in our land. This is difficult enough, let alone struggling for others.

AMILCAR CABRAL

Today the people who yesterday could express no views on their lives and on their destiny, can express their view, can make decisions. This is a clear evidence that the struggle is of our people, by our people and for our people.

AMILCAR CABRAL

It is impossible to struggle effectively for the independence of a people, unless we really know our reality and unless we really start out from that reality to wage the struggle.

AMILCAR CABRAL

For us, for our people and for our land, the time has come to put an end to indecisions and promises, to adopt definite action. We have already made too many sacrifices, but we are determined to make more to recover our freedom and human dignity, whatever the path to be followed.

AMILCAR CABRAL

A people's struggle is effectively theirs if the reason for that struggle is based on the aspirations, the dreams, the desire for justice and progress of the people themselves and not on the aspirations, dreams or ambitions of half a dozen persons who are in contradiction with the actual interests of their people.

AMILCAR CABRAL

We believe in the equality of races. We believe in the freedom of the people of all races. We believe in cooperation. In this struggle of ours, in this struggle to redeem Africa, we are fighting not against race and colour and creed. We are fighting against a system, a system which degrades and exploits.

AMILCAR CABRAL

Hundreds and thousands of us have died in many an imperialist war. If we die in the struggle of black emancipation it will be as men bringing into this world the wholesome, rich benefits of Black Power.

KWAME NKRUMAH

If, as everyone admits, white racism has blocked black aspiration since the beginning of the century then only a political struggle to compel respect for the black experience can compel change. Education alone can solve nothing, for the ultimate question concerns the political content of the education.

MARCUS GARVEY

We have taken the correct road, even though hazardous. We face death as we face life with head up, eyes lifted, proud and unafraid. The seed dies that life may spring forth. So we may meet death knowing that we cannot be defeated. For the oppressed people of the world will one day triumph.

KWAME NKRUMAH

The struggle for African freedom may be long and gloomy, but out of the cloud of suffering and disappointment loom the rays of hope and success on the distant horizon.

NNAMDI AZIKIWE

The decision has been made, the decision to fight for our freedom. Together we fight. It's your fight, it's my fight, it's our fight, it's the people's fight. If we cannot live our lives as free people then we will fight dying as people.

MARCUS GARVEY

We shall have to struggle for the right to create our own terms through which to define ourselves and our relationship to the society,and to have these terms recognised.This is the first necessity of a free people, and the first right that any oppressor must suspend.

STOKELY CARMICHAEL

Let every black American gird up his loins. We have crawled and pleaded for justice and we have been cheerfully spat upon and murdered and burned. We will not endure it forever. If we are to die, in God's name, let us perish like men and not like bales of hay.

W.E.B. DUBOIS

During my lifetime I have dedicated myself to this struggle of the African people. I have fought against white domination, and I have fought against black domination. I have cherished the ideal of a democratic and free society in which all persons live together in harmony and with equal opportunities. It is an ideal which I hope to live for and achieve. But if needs be, it is an ideal for which I am prepared to die.

NELSON MANDELA

For the African Dream is a tantalising dream that cannot be evaded, and it is up to us who live today to proclaim it everyday,everywhere, to fight for it and if necessary die for it, never allowing ourselves to carry the burden of insult and degradation or falsehood and treacherous cunning try to build a shelter for our dishonoured manhood.

MOKWUGO OKOYE

THE BLACK POWER.

A race without authority and power is a race
without respect. Power is the only argument that
satisfies man. Except the induvidual, the race, or
the nation, has POWER that is exclusive, it means
that individual, race, or nation, will be bound by
the will of the other who possesses this great
qualification.

MARCUS GARVEY

Man is not satisfied or moved by prayers or
petitions, but every man is moved by that power of
authority which forces him to do even against his
will.

MARCUS GARVEY

A State of rich and powerful men in which a
minority decides and imposes its will, whether we
agree or not, and whether we understand or not,
would be the continuation in a new form of the
situation against which we are struggling. The
question of people's power is the essential
question of our revolution.

SAMORA MOISES MACHEL

And so for us Black Power heralds, the long-awaited day od liberation from the shadows of obscurity. We take our place among the peoples of the world without hate or apologies, with confidence and with goodwill towards all men. The spectre of Black Power has taken shape and form, and its material presence fights to end the exploitation of man by man.

KWAME NKRUMAH

Black want to share power to bring about a world in which neither power nor dignity will be coloured black or white.

MARTIN LUTHER KING JNR

What the black man in Babylon needs is organised Black Power, and with that political power he can carve out his place in the sun and it won't be on a reservation or in the gas chamber.

ELDREDGE CLEAVER

These shackles must go. But that is but the beginning. The black man must have power; the power of men , the right to do , to know, to feel and to express that knowledge, action, and spiritual gift.

W.E.B. DUBOIS

Is the black man poor? Yes, but he isn't always going to be poor. Ignorant? Yes, but he isn't always going to be ignorant. The progress that he has already made in these directions shows clearly what the future is to be .Knowledge is power; wealth is power and that power the black man is getting.

F.S.GRIMBLE

However, we may twist our words and regardless of our personal feelings   the stark reality remains that the power necessary to end racism, colonialism, capitalism, and imperialism, will only come through long protracted, bloody, brutal and violent wars with our oppressors.

H.RAP BROWN.

The possibilities of black professionals will be great to the extent that the black people will allow their greatness. Their destiny is with the black race. The power that permanently lifts a people is within that people, so also the forces that degrade them.

PROF.JOSEPH BIBB

The Negro must get power of every kind. Power in education, science, industry, politics, and higher government. That kind of power that will stand out signnally, so that other races and nations can see, and if they will not see, then FEEL.

MARCUS GARVEY

Power concedes nothing wihtout demand. It never did and never will find out just what any people will quietly submit to and you have found out the exact measure of injustice and wrong which will be imposed upon them, and these will continue till they are resisted with either words or blow or with both. The limit of tyrants are described by the endurance of those whom they oppress.

FREDERICK DOUGLAS

Africa in world politics appears in a new light of dignity, considerable experience and solidality: a bloc to be recognised, a group to be reckoned with, knit together in co-operation and mutual supplementation. Africa will no longer be the Dark Continent. It will remain the Black Continent, but with its own formidable attribute   Black Power.

LAMBERT V.EJIOFOR

History rarely moves in a straight line; its course is uneven. Today as a result of the contradictions in capatilism, neo-colonialism and racism, Black Power is emerging on the stage of history. The oppressed of the earth are seeking a new way out to resolve these contradictions and achieve total emancipation.

KWAME NKRUMAH

Unless we who have power   whether political or technical   remain one with the masses, then we cannot serve them. Our opportunity is unparalleled in man's history, We must meet the challenge with courage, and with humility.

JULIUS NYERERE.

THE PRIDE OF THE BLACK RACE.

Give me back my black self to recover my courage
and my boldness to feel myself myself, a new self
from the one I was yesterday.
Yesterday without complication. Yesterday when the
hour of uprooting came.

DR.R.A.ARMATTOE

We are not fighting for the right to be like you.
We respect ourselves too much for that.When we advocate freedom, we mean freedom for us to be
black, or brown, and you to be white, and yet live
together in a free and equal society. Our fight is
not for racial sameness but for racial equality.

JOHN OLIVER KILLENS

There is no beauty in the world unless it looks
like me. I shall teach the Black Man to see beauty
in himself, to the exclusion of all others.

MARCUS GARVEY

The world has made being black a crime......
I hope to make it a virtue.

MARCUS GARVEY

I am a Negro and all a negro, I am black all over and proud of my beautiful black skin.

MAJOLA AGBEBE

If you could just be a nigger one Saturday night, you would never want to be a white man again as long as you live.

WILLIAM FAULKNER

I am a Negro, and I make not apology for being a Negro, because my God created me to be what I am. You can condemn my body, but not my soul.

MARCUS GARVEY

Great men have come out of Greece, out of Rome, out of Carthage, great men will come out of Africa, as they have done in the days of yore. Our only duty is to grasp the helm of opportunity, clear out deserts, conquer our mountains, remould our thinking and reconstruct our outlook, with an eye for Great Africa, so that we can look, with pride, the world in its face and say, "I am an African".

MARCUS GARVEY

Show me the race or nation without a flag, and I will show you a race of people without any pride.

MARCUS GARVEY

'...Africa is not an extension of any other continent...It devolves on us to establish our own African Community, geographically prescribed. That is why I consider that the step which we have taken is so important a step towards the establishement of this African Community, which will have its own distinctive outlook   an African Personality.

KWAME NKRUMAH

Be proud of your race today as our fathers were in the days of yore. We have a beautiful history, and we shall create another in the future that will astonish the world.

MARCUS GARVEY

The black people have freed themselves from the dead weight of the albatros of blackness that once hang about their neck. They have done it by picking it up in their arms and holding it out with pride for all the world to see. They have done it by embracing it not in the dark of the moon but in the searing light of the white sun. They have said "Yes" to it and found that the skin that was once seen as symbolising their shame is in reality their badge of honour.

SHIRLEY CHISHOLM

As I look at the past history of the black race I feel proud of my antecedents, proud of the glorious past which no amount of hate and prejudice could wipe from history's page.

MARCUS GARVEY

If I went to Heaven, and God said, "Aggrey, I am going to send you back, would you like to go as a white man?" I should reply, 'No, send me back as a black man, yes , completely black?' And if God should ask, "Why?", I would reply, 'Because I have a work to do as a black man that no white can do. Please send me back as black as you can make me. I am proud of my colour; whoever is not of his colour is not fit to live.'

DR.KWEGYRI AGGREY

The black man must find himself as a black man before he can find himself as an American.

JAMES L.FARMER

Merely by describing yourself as black you have started on a road towards emancipation, you have committed yourself to fight against all forces that seek to use your blackness as a stamp that marks you out as a subservient human being.

STEPHEN BIKO

Africa today brings a fresh civilisation to take root among the flourishing civilisation of the world, to cast a new focus on old problems and by its freshness help to evaluate them in a new light. But above all, Africa is a continent of new spirit and new endeavour in which the Negro people of the world can take pride and others can value and respect.

MARCUS GARVEY

I stand before you, a proud black man, honoured to be a black man, who would be nothing else in God's creation but a black man.

MARCUS GARVEY

If this and coming generations are taught to believe the crushing and slanderous dictum of natural inferiority, what hope is there for the salvation of the race, for a man can rise no higher than his ideal? For the black man to reach the height and possiblities that await him, he must learn to be proud of his race and colour. No race can be successful until it does things.

PROF.JOSEPH D.BIBB

An African nationality is the great desire of my
soul. I believe nationality to be an ordinance of
nature and no people can rise to an influential
position among nations without a distinct and
efficient nationality. Cosmopolitism never effec-
ted anything and never will.

E.W.BLYDEN

The knowledge that one is not alone...that the
struggle is an international struggle for the dignity of man, and that you are part of this family
of man   this alone sustains you.

WINNIE MANDELA

A people denied history is a people deprived of
dignity.

ALI A.MAZUVI.

Black Consciousness is to conquer a way of
feelings of black inferiority, to incalcate black
pride. It is a way of life, an attitude of mind ,
with the basic tenet that the black man must
reject all value systems that seek to make him a
foreigner in the country of his birth.

LAMBEDE.

THE DESTINY OF THE BLACK RACE

One nation is one ideal, one destiny is one secular faith in a better tomorrow for all Africans.

ARTHUR NWANKO

The people of Africa cannot continue to accept as their destiny the denial of human rights. We, too, have a right to live, to enjoy freedom and to pursue happiness like other human beings.

NNAMDI AZIKIWE

Black people must see liberation from the dominance and control of white society. Nothing less than this liberation will allow black people to determine their own destinies.

ROY INNIS

We are moving just now towards a point of no return in black and white America and it behoves all of us to re-examine our strategies and commitments and to ask ourselves where we are in time and where we want to go.

LERONE BENNETT JR

The countries of the third world recognise today the conditions which could permit them to enter upon the path of development and progress. They cannot be ignorant of the dark future which would be their destiny if they let slip away the opportunities that they now have for joining battle and making the efforts and sacrifices necessary for their well-being.

HOURI BOUMEDIENNE

Being subservient to the will and caprice of progressive races will not prove anything superior in us. Being satisfied to drink of the dregs from the cup of human progress will not demonstrate our fitness as a people to exist along side of others, but when of our own initiative we strike out to build industries, government, and ultimately empires, then and only then will we as a race, prove to our Creators, and to man in general, that we are fit to survive and capable of shaping our own destiny.

MARCUS GARVEY

The battle which is to decide the future role of blacks has begun. The struggle will be long and hard. All black men, educated and uneducated, sick and well, weak and strong, young and old must stand and fight. If we fail at this decisive moment, then our fate will be sealed forever.

MARCUS GARVEY

We are determined to maintain our mastery over our own destiny - to defend our national freedom. We are determined to change the condition of our lives. It is to meet these two needs that we must have both change and stability. These two must be interrelated for neither is possible without the other.

JULIUS NYERERE

We have no design to elbow out of South Africa anyone, but equally we have no intention whatsoever of abandoning our divine right of ourselves determining our destiny according to the holy and perfect plan of our Creator.

CHIEF ALBERT LUTHULI

Our destiny is in our hands. It is beginning to dawn upon us generally that if we would be saved, we must save ourselves. We have it to do or reap the bitter consequences. We have the ability and capacity to reach the highest point, even to go further in the march of progress than has been made by any people.

GEORGE L.KNOX

There are brief climatic periods in history when the destiny of whole peoples seems to resolve itself for better or for worse. The old gives way to the new; and the new goes forward with a force that is sudden and mysterious.

BASIL DAVIDSON

Hitherto we have been viewed and have viewed ourselves as an impotent and spiritless race, having only a mission of folly and degradation before us. Today we stand at the portals of a new world, a new life and destiny.

FREDERICK DOUGLAS

The individual, the race, the nation, that helps itself is helped by God. The individual, the race or nation that leaves its destiny to forces completely exterior is doomed, and in the destruction there is no remorse, there is no shedding of tears by anyone but the sufferer himself.

MARCUS GARVEY

If we want to turn Africa into a new Europe, then let us leave the destiny of our countries to Europeans. But if we want humanity to advance a step farther, if we want to bring it up to a different level than that which Europe has shown it, then we must invent and we must make discoveries.

FRANTZ FANON

The launching of the struggles and the victories we have won reveal concretely that there is no such thing as fateful destiny; we are capable of transforming society and creating a new life.

SAMORA MOISES MACHEL

The possibilities of black professionals will be great to the extent that the black people will allow their greatness.
Their destiny is with the black race. The power that permanently lifts a people is within that people, so also the forces that degrade them.

PROF.JOSEPH BIBB

We are not asking charity of you, because we believe in self-help; we believe that as a race of people struggling onward and upward we must of ourselves lift ourselves up; and all we ask you is that you treat us kindly and decently.

MARCUS GARVEY

We will never be able to reason for ourselves unless we learn to think for ourselves. The thinking mind is the active mind, and the active mind is the growing man; the growing mind moves the man, and the man that moves helps to move the world.

J.R. HAWKINS

The reliance of our race upon the progress and achievements of others for a consideration in sympathy, justice and rights is like a dependence upon a broken stick, resting upon which will eventually consign you to the ground.

MARCUS GARVEY

Let the black man start out seriously to help himself and ere the fall of many more decades you will see him a new man, once more fit for the association of the 'gods' and the true companionship of those whose respect he lost.

MARCUS GARVEY

The best of a race does not live on the patronage and philantropy of others, but makes an effort to do for itself.

MARCUS GARVEY

But for his industry, perseverance, endurance and docility he could never have climbed as far as he has on the ladder of progress. The black man is fast learning that if he would be free he, himself, must strike the blow. The heights are still beyond, but he is slowly rising, and day by day hope grows brighter. May God continue this progress until he shall stand shoulder to shoulder with the highest civilisation and culture of the world.

REV. DANIEL W. DAVIS

The love of self and self-respect along with the will to do something for self, if given a chance, will get you the respect of all civilised nations. Love and unity of self is the key to our salvation.

ELIJAH MUHAMMAD

The individual, the race, the nation, that helps
itself is helped by God. The individual, the race
or nation that leaves its destiny to forces completely exterior is doomed,and in the destruction
there is no remorse, there is no shedding of tears
by anyone but the sufferer himself.

MARCUS GARVEY

The black man must be up and doing if he will
break down the prejudice of the rest of the world.
Prayer alone is not going to improve our condition,nor the policy of watchful waiting. We must
strike out for ourselves in the course of material
achievement, and by our own effort and energy
present to the world those forces by which the
progress of man is judged.

MARCUS GARVEY

As African, we must exercise the freedom of
choice. The choice is between African life and
European death.A choice between Africa and Europe.
The conditions are clear cut as this. We can no
longer sacrifice ourselves for a bit of crumbs off
the master's table.
We have to build our own table. Not only that, we
have to make our own table. Not only that, we have
to make and bake our own bread. moreover, the
bread must be African. Neither are we going to buy
or borrow the flour, the wheat will be planted on
African soil by African hands.

DR. ABRAHAM JEROME

It was to be expected that the first black nations emerging from slavery would exhibit to a painful degree the spirit of dependence, an inclination to lean on something and on somebody. Gradually, however, the black man is realising the importance of self-help, self-respect, self-reliance and the ambition to be and to do. Many agencies will deepen this impression, and ultimately lead him to imbibe in all its fullness the sentiment of the poet - 'Destiny is not about thee, but within; Thyself must make thyself'.

PROF. W.H. CROGMAN

The negro will never be able to hold up his head as a man and speak as a man until he is able to do things that other races have done and are doing. This is the urge that forces men on to the accomplishment of those things that are worthwhile, and it is hoped that the African at home as well as the African abroad will work toward that end.

MARCUS GARVEY

We aim to define and encourage a new consciousness among black people which will make it possible for us to proceed toward those answers and those solutions to our problem.

STOKELEY CARMICHAEL

Black people must redefine themselves, and only they can do that. Throughout this country, vast segments of the black communities are beginning to recognise the need to assert their own definitions, to reclaim their history, their culture; to create their own sense of community and togetherness.

STOKELEY CARMICHAEL

Our destiny is in our own hands. It is beginning to dawn on us generally, that if we would be saved, we must save ourselves. We have it to do or reap the very bitter consequences. We have the ability and capacity to reach the highest point, and even to go further in the march of progress than has been made by any people.

GEORGE L. KNOX

Before this century shall have ended, the black man through his own manly efforts, aided by his friends, shall reach that point in the world of civilisation, where he will be recognised and treated as any other world citizen.

DR. D.W. GULP

The past and our limited achievements give us
assurance of glorious possibilities to come. Just
how far and to what extent we are to realise the
fruition of our cherished dreams of rising to the
full height of honourable manhood rests chiefly
with us.

PROF.T. DE S. TUCKER

We have passed the stage where we can talk
seriously of whites acting toward black out of
moral imperatives. That does not work. Yet we can
still talk of change coming about through enlightened self-interest, the prime motivator of
orderly change in society throughout the history
of mankind. That is the only thing that works
without destroying what it seeks to save.

ROY INNIS

Our enemies,triumphant for the present, are
fighting the stars in their course. Justice and
humanity must prevail. We live to tell these dark
brothers of ours - scattered in counsel, wavering
and weak - that no bribe of money or notoriety, no
promise of wealth or fame, is worth the surrender
of a people's manhood or the loss of a man's self-
respect. We are men;we will be treated as men. On
this rock we have planted our banners. We will
never give up through the trump of doom find us
still fighting.

W.E.B. DUBOIS

It is only in proportion as the black man becomes interested in himself that he enlists the interest of others, and only in proportion as he respects himself that he commands the respect of others.

PROF. W.H. CROGMAN

It is a hopeful sign that the black man is beginning, with some degre of seriousness, to turn his eyes inward, to study himself, and try to discover what are his possibilities, and what obstructions that lie in the way to his larger developments.

PROF. W.H. CROGMAN

The black man has reached beyond the slave stage ! He is no longer content with being a passive observer, a quiet looker-on, while his character and interests are under discussion. He is now disposed to speak for himself, to 'take part in the conflict'.

PROF. W.H. CROGMAN

The independence of a nation must be told, or it does not exist at all. Without economic independence there can be only a limited degree of political, social, cultural, or even military independence.

JULIUS NYERERE

THE SURVIVAL OF THE BLACK RACE.

We have passed through the furnace and have not yet been consumed. During more than two centuries and a half, we have survived contact with the white race. We have risen from the small number of twenty to he large number of five millions, living and increasing where other tribes are decreasing and dying.

FREDERICK DOUGLAS

Black survival is at stake, and we black people must define and assert the conditions necessary for our being-in-the-world. Only we can decide how much we can endure from the racists. And as we make our decision in the midst of life and death, being and nonbeing, the role of Black Theology is to articulate this decision by pointing to the revelation of God in the black liberation struggle.

J.H.CONE

Survival as a person means not only food and shelter, but also belonging to a community that remembers and understands the meaning of its past.

TOM MBOYA

Black people in Africa, America, and the West Indies, have survived slavery, colonialism, and imperialism. Today we can survive change.

We have been oppressed as people, and have been divided to the point of taking roots in different cultures. But as we struggle to achieve our full liberation, these differences should become less important.

TOM MBOYA

In spite of the enormity of the problems of nation-building and our failure in the past in tackling them, salvation is somewhere down the street of Time. We can hope for no more.

MOKWUGO OKOYE

In these days of struggle for racial survival, let us bear no malice; let us be charitable and stand firm in the cause of justice and righteousness. God knows we hate none on account of race or colour, but we love our continent, and we want our countries to be free, and we shall be free.

NNAMDI AZIKIWE

The black people have got to survive or be destroyed by white people. For a black man to survive against the white races undying sacrifice must be the first instinct. And this sacrifice will have to be the embodiment of every single concept inluding bloodshed or death in this struggle for survival.

W.E.B.DUBOIS

The African people are beginning to realise that in their struggle for survival in today's world, their desire for cultural authenticity must be infused with modern technology. For culture itself is a dynamic thing and bound by the two coordinates of time and place.

ARTHUR NWANKO

The road is long,the struggle will be immense, but the survivor of slave trade, of colonial pillage and massacres, will not lack determination, the courage and the will to live.

SERGIO VIEIRA

You can enslave the bodies of men, you can shackle the hands of men, the feet of men, you can imprison the bodies of men, but you cannot shackle or imprison the minds of men.

MARCUS GARVEY

Let us not deceive ourselves at our situation in this country. Weighted with a heritage or moral iniquity from our past history, hard pressed in the economic world by foreign immigrants and native prejudice, hated here, despised there and pitied everywhere; our one haven of refuge is ourselves, and but one means of advance, our own belief in our great destiny, our own implicit trust in our ability and worth.

W.E.B.DUBOIS

Man's struggle for survival is a clash between cultures. The strength of a man depends entirely upon the strenth of his culture.
Survival is culture. It is the link between man and his God. Africa cannot serve two masters. Let us render unto Caesar the things that are Caesar's, and unto God the things that are God's. The European civilisation is Africa's Caesar. We cannot serve both. By serving European Christianity we are destroying our own cultural links with our God. Man must have faith, but this must be a faith within, not without. As Africans, we cannot possibly have faith in Europe.

DR.ABRAHAM JEROME

We shall be saved someday despite our diffi-
culties.For though, like other people,we in Africa
have had our dark ages marked by primitive productive techniques,our darkness recedes perhaps too
slowly but surely.
And in the lightening landscape we begin to see
ourselves more clearly as a kindly, hopeful, and
descent people who even in the midst of injustice
and misfortune remain intensely loyal to everyone
bound to us.

MOKWUGE OKOYE

We have only started; we have just made the first
lap in the great race for existence, and for a
place in the political and economic sun of men.

MARCUS GARVEY

So in Africa, where men have absorbed and diffused
ideas since the world began, we cannot now retreat
into a cocoon of self-conceited isolation and
still expect to survive in the modern world.

MOKWUGO OKOYE

The American Negro demands equality, industrial
equality and social equality; and he is never
going to rest satisfied with anything less. He
demands this in no spirit of braggadocio and with
no obsequious envy of others, but as an absolute
measure of self-defence and the only one that will
assure to the darker races their ultimate survival
on earth.

W.E.B.DUBOIS.

Dangers and difficulties have not deterred us in
the past; they will not frighten us now. But we
must be prepared for them like men who mean
business and who do not waste energy in vain talk
and idle action.

NELSON MANDELA.

We have survived slavery, colonialism and imperialism. We can survive change.
Indeed we welcome change, for it is the concept of
change that we pursue our efforts for a better
life for our people.

TOM MBOYA

THE BLACK RACE ACTION.

What is wanted now is action. Let us all, through
our concerted action build upon the solid
foundations laid for us by the illustrious fathers
of Pan Africanism, strive to build for ourselves
and our future program, the better world that our
oppressors have completely failed even to conceive. We have a duty to perform. Let us each go
home and do it. We are our own liberators. Let us
be free tomorrow, alive or even did.

                                    JUMBA ABBOUD

We will not stand by and be satisfied with
resolutions and prayers, or with acts of charity by
men and women of goodwill who partake of the
advantages of the system while pretending to
sympathise with us.

                               OLUSEGUN OBASANJO

We have taken too much and pined too long over our
disabilities   political, social, economic; and it
is now time that we embark on constitutional
positive steps to achieve positive results.

                                 KWAME NKRUMAH

Action! Action! not criticism, is the plain duty of this hour. The office of speech now is only to point out when, where, and how to strike to the best advantage. There is no time to delay. The tide is at its flood that leads on to fortune. From East to West, from North to South, the sky is written all over, 'Now or Never'!

MARCUS GARVEY

Awake, awake, put on thy strength. Africa, awake! Put on the beautiful robes of Pan-African socialism. You have a continent to regain! You have freedom and human dignity to attain!

W.E.B.DUBOIS

We cannot wait until we are encompassed by our doom for failing to seize this grand opportunity rising to the call of Africa's finest hour. We cannot, we must not, we dare not fail or falter.

KWAME NKRUMAH

The time comes in the life of any nation when there remains only two choices - submit or fight. That time has now come to South Africa. We shall not submit and we have no choice but to hit back by all means in our power in defence of our people, our future, and our freedom.

NELSON MANDELA

Africa must refuse to be humiliated, exploited, and pushed any more. And with the same determination we must refuse to humiliate, exploit or push others around. We must act, not just say words.

JULIUS NYERERE

The time for drawing up plans is now past. Africa today must act. The peoples of Africa are waiting impatiently for such action to begin. Africa Unity and Solidarity are no longer mere dreams; we must now embody them in concrete decisions.

PATRICK LUMUMBA

Africa cannot wait any more, for we have been waiting too long. Africa cannot be silent, for we have been silenced too long. Africa cannot take dictations any more, for we have been dictated to for too long. The time is past when we have no say in deciding our destinies. Now times have changed. If we, in this generation fail then we have not only failed this generation but also our sons and daughters yet unborn.

MARCUS GARVEY

Now we, the black men have started to speak and I am only the forerunner of an awakened Africa that shall never go back to sleep.

MARCUS GARVEY

Dangers and difficulties have not deterred us in the past; they will not frighten us now. But we must be prepared for them like men who mean business and who do not waste energy in vain talk and idle action.

NELSON MANDELA

Unfortunately, we are living in contemporary times, in a shrinking world where isolation is impossible and we cannot afford to take a couple of centuries trying to catch up with the rest of the world.

ARTHUR NWANKO

Evidently one of the first things to be done by which the black man could be reconstructed and become an intelligent member of society is to educate him; make him more provident and painstaking; teach him the value of time, of money and the intimate relationship of the two.

JOSEPHINE S. YATES

Today all Africans believe that the greatness of the Continent, is the greatness of Africans, and for this reason we see, with immense joy, the profitable work destined to achieve the greatness of Africa. The day has really come when Africa begins her forward march and nothing will stop her, till she has reached the summit of glory.

KWAME NKRUMAH

The prejudices that we have lived with for so long, the false classification of the human race into masters and servants are some of the graet historical frauds of our time. We can only refute and reject them by our actions; by doing all we can to erase the foundations of this division. Self-confidence lies in our strength, in our spirit, that rejects enslavement - mental and otherwise.

ARTHUR NWANKO

We shall not ask England or France or Italy or Belgium, " Why are you here ? " We shall only command them " Get out of here ".

MARCUS GARVEY

In order to achieve real action, you must yourself be a living part of Africa and of her thought; you must be an element of that popular energy which entirely calls forth for the freeing, the progress and the happiness of African. There is no place for the artist or for the intellectual who is himself concerned with and completely at one with the people in the great battle of Africa and of suffering of humanity.

SEKOU TOURE

I cannot believe that all of us who are here will fail South Africa because we are cowards and apathetic.
I believe we all will do our best - whatever the difficulties are - for the realisation of this glorious democratic South Africa we dream of.

CHIEF ALBERT LUTHULI

Men of America, the problem is plain before you. Here is a race transplanted through the criminal foolishness of your fathers. Whether you like it or not the millions are here, and here they will remain. If you do not lift them up, they will pull you down.

W.E.B. DUBOIS

The only time we have is now. So now we must demand the impossible. Now we must struggle for the impossible. Now we must live for the impossible. Now we must die for the impossible. Only then will it burst into the realm of the possible. Only then will our bright and morning star replace the rocket's red glare. Only then will our sons and daughters be free.

VICENT HARDING

Let us reinforce our rank and file in the fight
for freedom, no longer suffering in silence and
whinning like a helpless dog, but striking back
with all the force at our command when we are
struck, preferring to suffer the consequences of
pressing forward our claim to a legacy of freedom
to surrender our legacy to despoilers and
usurpers.

NNAMDI AZIKIWE

We are moving just now toward a point of no return
in black and white America and it behoves all of
us to re-examine our strategies and commitments
and to ask ourselves where we are in time and
where we want to go.

LERONE BENNETT JR

THE BLACK REVOLUTION.

For us in Africa, for the people of African descent everywhere, there can be no turning back, no compromise, no fear or failure or death. Africa must fulfil her destiny. Even though revolution in other parts of the world may wither or go astray, the African Revolution must reach its goal of unity and socialism.

KWAME NKRUMAH

The African Revolution begins with a consciousness of Africa by Africans for Africa, with a specific identity, history, culture , conception of life and social organisation.
This conscious African is aware of his obligations, duties, and responsibilities to his faith and kin, in respect to human dignity, freedom , and self-reliance in Africa, of Africa, by Africans, for Africa.

CHUBA OKADGIBO

You can jail a revolutiornary, but you cannot jail revolution.

BOBBY SEALE

A revoluton is a historical process and at each historical juncture we have to act in conformity with given objective conditions of time.

J.J.Rawlings

The African Revolution is not inspired by mere love of Revolution. It is inspired by the gross inequalities of our continent and our desire to eradicate these inequalities.

KWAME NKRUMAH

To take part in the African revolution, it is not enough to write a revolutionary song; you must fashion the revolution with the people. And if you fashion it with the people, the songs will come by themselves, and of themselves.

SEKOU TOURE

We must not, we cannot, ignore the fact that the Revolution has to accommodate a range of views and opinions. Whilst we shall never compromise our principles, We must at the same time keep open the doors of dialogue in an atmosphere of frankness.

J.J.RAWLINGS

Revolution is the pre-eminent characteristic of our time. There is not one revolution; there are many. Sometimes, they are tangential to each other. At other times, they surge together for a while like the overflow of separate rivers at flood stage.

C.ERIC LINCOLN

The impossibble through struggle becomes the probable, and the probable becomes reality.

MANNING MARABLE

As each new attempt is made to divide us and to divert us from our purpose, it must be exposed and attacked. Already the ordinary men and women in Africa are talking the language of the African Revolution. They speak of freedom, unity, and socialism, and know that these objectives are synonymous.

JULIUS NYERERE

Suspicion and distrust of those who do not always think identically with us will not help the Revolutionary process. All those whose goal is to secure a just society should be limited by that goal, and not divided by bickering over the exact path to take.

J.J.RAWLINGS

The liberation of women is not an act of charity. It is not the result of a humanitarian or compassionate position. It is a fundamental necessity for the Revolution, a guarantee of its continuity, and a condition for its success.

SAMORA MOISES MACHEL

Life for us in the conflict ahead is all stern and serious. Wounds and scars will for generations yet to come be the decorations for our leaders in thought and action.

PROF.T.DE TUCKER

Today people have set in motion a revolutionary hurricane to put an end to exploitation of man by man. Eventually, imperialism and racialism will become merely a chapter in the history of men.

JULIUS NYERERE

The world still belongs to the nationalists. We, who incorrectly regard ourselves as beyond or in some sense too old for nationalism cannot deny it to others by pretending it is always outmoded or dangerous. Every person needs the consciousness that is part of an efficacious order, and that when it is threatened, men will come to lead, inspire, to articulate what must be done to preserve it or establish a new order.

JULIUS NYERERE

Countrymen, we have committed ourselves to a revolutionary transformation of our society. That we shall never go back.
We must remind both our critics and admirers that revolution is not a one act play which happens once and it's all over.

J.J.RAWLINGS

THE BLACK MAN'S ABILITIES, QUALITIES & CAPACITIES

Give us a chance to live in ease as you are living, so that we may have a chance to bring out those latent, hidden powers which made a Newton, which gave us a Darwin and a Huxley. We are capable of giving such men to the world if we are forced into the corner to think.

MARCUS GARVEY

The better negro is not, as a rule, seen; his works, as a rule not known; his refinement, his morals and industry are not advertised, hence a wrong notion as to the bend and the intent of the race is noised abroad.

GEORGE L. KNOX

We are going to show the world what the black man can do when he works in freedom and we are going to make this Continent the focal point for the development of the world.

PATRICK LUMUMBA

Despite all theories and all disparagements, the negro is a man. By every fact, by every argument, by every rule of measurement, in mental, moral or spiritual, by everything in the heavens above and in the earth beneath which vindicates the humanity of any class of beings, the negro's humanity is equally vindicated.

FREDERICK DOUGLAS

The best in a race is not reflected through or by the action of its apes, but by its ability to create of and by itself.

MARCUS GARVEY

If our race expects to meet the possibilities we must learn what it takes to make true characters. It is not the exhibit from the outside, it is what we are, as we are judged from our actions, by the fruits we bring forth.

GEORGE L. KNOX

In spite of white exploitation, we are still a nation. It may be a miserable, mangled, tortured, twisted tertium or to quote a higher authority,'a nation scattered and peeled..............a Nation melted out and trodden down, but still a Nation'. We have a Nation and what is more we have a Past - 'Though ungraced in history'.

KWAME NKRUMAH

While it is not sensible to shut our eyes to these painful reminders of the obstacles to our progress, while it is even best to invite a searching scrutiny of them to the end that they may be torn off by heroic methods, if need be, after all an occasional study of our strong parts is a help in the struggle.

PROF T. DE S. TUCKER

The twentieth century has shown that the black man has ceased to be a thing, a commodity that could be bought and sold, a mere animal; he is indeed a human possessing all the qualities of mind and heart that belong to the rest of mankind, capable of receiving education and imparting it to his fellow man, able to think, act, feel and develop those intellectual and moral qualities, such as characterise mankind generally.

MARY B. TALBORT

Shunted to the right and left, with our path continually obstructed, and our ambition jeered at, we have kept quietly and persistently on, until we can now show we are sufficiently powerful to be regarded as a force.

J.PORTER

165

That our nature will be largely modified by the necessities of our growth must be an accepted fact, but our merit, worth and fitness in the world will substantially be the product of our qualities as they are today.

PROF T.DE S. TUCKER

It is always right for one to strike for one's own liberty. Blacks must look around themselves, and not afar, for the instruments and forces that must be utilized for their salvation.
Neither institution nor friends can make a race stand unless it has strength in its own legs. Races like individuals must stand or fall by their own merits. It is only through struggle and the surmounting of difficulties that races, like individuals are made strong, powerful and useful. this is the road the black man should travel; This is the road,I think the black man will travel

JULIUS NYERERE

Many historic races who have dominated mankind, made less rapid progresss than we, at the point we have reached. This remarkable advancement may be ascribed in the main to the superior attributes which give us a flexible and well balanced temperament.

PROF. T. DE S. TUCKER

If the African is unable to teach the outside world something of the inner feelings of his people; if, for some reason or other, he can show nothing of his real self to those anxious to learn,and to sssist him; if he cannot make his friends feel the force of his racial character and sympathise with his racial aspiration, then it is evident that his education has been sadly defective.

MARCUS GARVEY

The negro needs a nation and a country of his own where he can best show evidence of his own ability in the art of human progress. Scattered as an unmixed and unrecognised part of alien nations and civilisations is but to demonstrate his imbecility, and point him out as an unworthy derelict, fit neither for society of Greek,Jew, nor Gentile.

MARCUS GARVEY

God has endowed us with the capacity to suffer and undergo the trials incident to race development. If we can recognise the need for this training, severe though it be, if we do not chafe and fume and fret and get angry because our deliverance has not come, we may well be comforted in the meanwhile that any device of man to deny us a share in the government of a common heritage in this land consecrated by heaven to suffering humanity, will prove a complete failure.

PROF .T. DE S. TUCKER

Greece gave the world beauty; Rome gave us power, but in the African people there is the great gushing water of love, which will develop wonders for the world.

REV. S. KERR

The negro is also thinking in terms of per- petual motion; the negro is also thinking in terms of hidden mysteries of the world; and you do not know what the oppressed and suppressed negro, by virtue of his condition and circumstances, may give to the world as a surprise.

MARCUS GARVEY

If we want to turn Africa into a new Europe, then let us leave the destiny of our countries to Europeans. But if we want humanity to advance a step further, if we want to bring it up to a different level than that which Europe has shown it, then we must invent and we must make discoveries.

FRANTZ FANON

We are going to show the world what the black man can do when he works in freedom and we are going to make this Continent the focal point for the development of the world.

PATRICK LUMUMBA

The Third World today faces Europe like a colossal mass whose aim should be to try to resolve the problems to which Europe has not been able to find the answers.

FRANTZ FANON

Be not dismayed.....Africa's sun is steadily and surely rising and shall soon shed its rays around the world. Steady yourselves and go forward.

MARCUS GARVEY

The modern world needs remember that in this age, when the ends of the world are being brought so near together the millions of black men in Africa, America and the islands of the sea, not to speak of the myriads elsewhere, are bound to have great influence upon the world in the future by reason of sheer memebers and physical contact.

W.E.B. DUBOIS

Our lives are not coloured by daily obsessions with East versus West. At a time when the world is old, and the thoughts of the great developed nations have broken through the bounds of space, which could well lead to universal obstruction, we in Africa are creating something new.

TOM MBOYA

Africa rejects a world economic model wherein power is manipulated by a few countries, who legitimise their civilising mission and project themselves as bearers of modern technology, who bring redemption to the backward countries. We want a New Interna-tional Economic Order, where an effective African participation in decision-making will be guaranteed.

CHUBA OKADGIBO

The race needs workers at this time, not plagiarists, copyists and mere imitators; but men and women who are able to create, to originate and improve, and thus make an independent racial contribution to the world and civilisation.

MARCUS GARVEY

The end is not in our day but in our time we can make certain contribution toward it. Let us not turn back, let us hold on, so that when the final history of man is to be written, there will not be glory for others but there will be glory for us.

MARCUS GARVEY

Africa is ripe enough to answer the call of the century. World powers have gone warlike and may soon, if left alone, sacrifice humanity for future power. For them humans are getting nearer to nothing. Africa, which before had led in civilisation, should move in to restore peace and harmony, to mediate and arbitrate, to break down mountains of armament, to procure collective security for all, and, to RESTORE THE DIGNITY OF MAN.

LAMBERT U. EJIOFOR

A nation that refuses to keep its rendezvous with history, that does not believe to be the bearer of a unique message - that nation is finished, ready to be placed in museum...Let the Negro African speak: above all, let him act. Let him bring like a leaven his message to the world in order to help build a universal civilisation.

LEOPOLD SENGHOR

With an informed mind, a skilful hand, and an upright conduct, there is no reason why the black man should not take his place upon the stage of action, play well his part in the drama of life, and meritoriously receive the plaudits of gazing nations of the world.

PROF. ARTHUR RICHARDSON

Our tasks are clear... We have to play our full part as world citizens in the development of humanity; to do that we have to shake off the mental effect upon ourselves of colonialism and discrimination. We have to fight colour prejudice and discrimination everywhere; and we have to assert, and where possible promote the rights of all the world's citizens for an equal share of the world's resources.

JULIUS NYERERE

Africa today brings a fresh civilisation to take root among the flourishing civilisation of the world, to cast a new focus on old problems and by its freshness help to evaluate them in a new light. But above all Africa is a continent of new spirit and new endeavour in which the Negro people of the world can take pride and others can value and respect.

MARCUS GARVEY

Black men want to share power to bring about a world in which neither power nor dignity will be coloured Black or White.

MARTIN LUTHER KING,JNR

THE BLACK CULTURE

Man's struggle for survival is a clash between cultures. The strength of a man depends entirely upon the strength of his culture. Survival is culture. It is the link between man and his God. Africa cannot serve two monsters. Let us render unto Caesar the things that are Caesar's, and unto God the things that are God's. The European civilisation is Africa's Caesar. We cannot serve both. By serving European Christianity we are destroying our own cultural links with our God. Man must have faith, but this must be a faith within not without. As Africans we cannot possibly have faith in Europe.

DR. ABRAHAM JEROME

A people who free themselves from foreign domination will not be culturally free unless, without underestimating the importance of positive contributions from the oppressor's culture and other cultures, they return to the upwards paths of their own culture.

AMILCAR CABRAL

Somewhere ahead there beckons a civilisation, a culture, which will take its place in the parade of God's history beside other great human syntheses, Chinese, Jewish, European. It will not necessarily be all black, but it will be African.

CHIEF ALBERT LUTHULI

In the ancient times, Europe looked to Africa for
new ideas for fresh inspirations, and the saying
was perpetuated and handed down from generation to
generation 'Semper aliquid novi ex Africa' - There
is always something new from Africa.

> Now lies she there,
> And none so poor to do her reverence.

All because thinking in our age has become a lost
Art.

REV. J.M. COX

We cannot confront the European Culture with gun
power and win. Our only hope is for us to use our
African Culture and thought power to unite ourselves and overwhelm the European culture.

BARBARA MAKEDA LEE

Our cultural identity and common historical
destiny should be our main concern as we have all
been treated unjustly by exploiting powers. We
should be able to identify ourselves, not by the
colour of our skin, which is a static element, but
solely in trems of our goods which are just and
noble.

SEKOU TOURE

Now if we are to make an independent nation - a strong nation - we must listen to the songs of our unsophisticated brethren, as they sing of their history,as they tell of their traditions,of the wonderful and mysterious events of their national life. We shall in this way, get back the strength of the race.

E.W. BLYDEN

One can escape the fact that the culture shared by the majority group in any given society must ultimately determine the broad direction taken by the joint culture of that society. This need not cramp the style of those who feel differently but on the whole, a country in Africa, in which the majority of people are African must inevitably exhibit African values and be truly African in style.

STEPHEN BIKO

We should go down to the grassroots of our culture, not to remain there, not to be isolated there,but to draw strength and substance therefrom, and with whatever additional sources of strength and material we acquire, proceed to set up a new form of society raised to the level of human progress.

SEKOU TOURE

175

The struggle, in the face of obstacles and in a variety of forms, reflects the awareness or grasp of a complete identity,generalises and consolidates the sense of dignity,strengthened by the development of political consciousness, and derives from the culture or cultures of the masses in revolt one of its principal strengths.

AMILCAR CABRAL

The African people are beginning to realise that in their struggle for survival in today's world, their desire for cultural authenticity must be infused with modern technology. For culture itself is a dynamic thing and bound by the two coordinates of time and place.

ARTHUR A. NWANKO

PROGRESS, DEVELOPMENT & RECONSTRUCTION OF THE BLACK RACE

We have made tremendous progress in our march,
though we are still unpleasant and selfish and
cruel and the ground gained one day may be lost in
another. Our world is still imperfect in many
ways; there are both bright and dark spots in many
places, and sometimes our best efforts are mocked
by fate and our gossamer dreams are blasted by
brute facts or the evil mechanism of social life.
Yet it is possible to see the silver lining
progress right through the long and dismal record
of selfishness and man's inhumanity to his fellow
man. Life, after all is a search, not a certainty,
and what everyone is seeking is fulfilment of his
positive potentialities in fruitful relationship
with other people.

MOKWUGO OKOYE

Necessity is not only the mother of invention, but
the soul of the law of progress-genius of civilization. It is here in the closing period of the
Twentieth Century effulgent with the light of all
the historic past and marvelous achievements that
the black man must stand or fall. Here in the
wilderness where peaks of cultivated mountaintops
in the near distance invite him onward and upward;
here under the full ordered sun of the brightest
day the world has seen he must work out his
salvation with fear and trembling.

PROF. JOSEPH D. BIBB

The advancement of man uncomprisingly demands a
ceaseless synthesis of ideas, a blending of ways
of living, a give and take of beliefs, and above
all a willingness to believe that the best is yet
to be.

DUNDIZE CHIZINIA

The essence of development along your own lines is
that you must have the right to develop and the
right to determine how to develop.
It's essence is freedom and - beyond freedom -
self-determination. This is the vision we hold for
our future and our development.

CHIEF ALBERT LUTHULI

We are to take no steps backward in our progress
in the opening days in the dawn of a new century.
A thinking people is a prosperous people.We are to
be measured by what we can accomplish,not by the
colour of the skin, the texture of the hair, the
colour of the eye or the contours of the head. But
we are to be measured as skilled farmers,
scholars, and artists.

N.W. HARLLEE

The developing countries face the challenge of
development.There is no alternative but to prosecute the task of development with resolution in
the knowledge that independence would be reduced
to a mere slogan if this challenge is not met
boldly.

TOM MBOYA

Today we have climbed the heights where we would open at least the outer courts of knowledge to all, display its treasures to many, and select the few to whom its mystery of truth is revealed, not wholly by birth or the accidents of the stock market, but at least in part according to deftness and aim, talent and character.

W.E.B. DUBOIS

Progress of and among any people will advance them in respect and appreciation of the rest of their fellows. It is such a progress that the black man must attach to himself if he is to rise above the prejudice of the world.

MARCUS GARVEY

The work of the Universal Negro Improvement Association is clear and clean cut. It is that of inspiring an unfortunate race with pride in self and with the determination of going ahead in creation of those ideals that will lift them to the unprejudiced company of races and nations. There is no desire for hate or malice, but every wish to see all mankind linked into a common fraternity of progress and achievement that will wipe away the odour of prejudice, and elevate the human race to the height of real godly love and satisfaction.

MARCUS GARVEY

The conditions under which we work and live are changing.Promising prospects are opening up before us.We are on the verge of a new nation;a new horizon opens before all of us as a people and we are determined never to fail.

JULIUS NYERERE

If the black man was indifferent to education; if he was actually getting poorer, then we might lose heart; but thank God, the very opposite is true. His face is in the right direction. He may not be pressing on as rapidly as some of us might wish to see him, but it is a matter for congratulation, that he is not retrograding, nor even standing still, but is moving on.

F.J. GRIMBLE

The time must surely come when South Africa must emerge from the dark night of racial fanaticism to take its place among the free nations of the world.

CHIEF ALBERT LUTHULI

It is not enough to say that we, the black people, have faculties. It is not sufficient to say that there lives in us the power to see, to hear, to feel,to reason,to think and to act;we must develop these powers until we can feel the benefit of the blessings that come from their use.

W.E.B. DUBOIS

We do not want to catch up with anyone. What we want to do is go forward all the time, night and day, in the company of Man, in the company of all men.

FRANZ FANON

Many historic races who have dominated mankind, made less rapid progress than we, at the point we have reached. This remarkable advancement may be ascribed in the main to the superior attributes which give us a flexible and well balance temperament.

PROF. T. DE TUCKER

This is Africa's age. This is the dawn of her fulfilment - the beginning of the climb to sublimity.

CHIEF ALBERT LUTHULI

Progress is peace,and peace is time for food, homes,for love, health,for hapiness, and books to read.

W.E.B. DUBOIS

Progress is the attraction that moves humanity, and to whatever people or race this modern virtue attracts itself, there will you find the splendour of pride and self-esteem that never fail to win the respect and admiration of all.

MARCUS GARVEY

Progress,of course,has occurred but is embedded in
the nature of things, not automatic and not bound
to occur always in the future. It is even well to
remind ourselves that there is still no Civilisation but several civilisations, no Humanity but
only different sorts of humanity, no Reason but
only different modes and kinds of thinking.

MOKWUGO OKOYE

A new civilisation, a new culture, shall spring up
from among our people, and the Nile shall once
again flow through the land of science of art and
of literature, wherein will live black men of the
highest learning and the highest accomplishment.

MARCUS GARVEY

We are running against time in Africa. Not only
have we to eliminate or eradicate the deficiencies
of our past, but we must also in the shortest
possible time attempt to catch up with modern
techniques.

KWAME NKRUMAH

Progress in the enjoyment of all the privileges
that will come to us must be the result of severe
and constant struggle rather than of artificial
forcing.

BOOKER T. WASHINGTON

We are now face to face with a new order of
things.Under this new regime we witness the fore-
shadow of a higher sense of civilisation, a higher
standard of morals, a broader field of culture and
a purer realm of thought.

J.R. HAWKINS

As the old nationalism dies with the imperialism
that bred it, there is a need to look for a model
of development ideas more suited to the times in
which we live and capable of giving the nation a
sense of purpose and direction.

MOKWUGO OKOYE

A people's struggle is effectively theirs if the
reason for that struggle is based on the aspirations, the dreams, the desire for justice and progress of the people themselves and not on the
aspirations, dreams or ambitions of half a dozen
persons who are in contradiction with the actual
interests of their people.

AMILCAR CABRAL

I can see springing up, cities of Africa becoming
the metropolis of science and learning architec-
ture and philosophy.And the immortal are resoun-
ding the echo: seek ye first the political kingdom
and all things shall be added unto you.

KWAME NKRUMAH

But for his industry, perseverance, endurance and docility he could never have climbed as far as he has on the ladder of progress. The black man is fast learning that if he would be free he,himself, must strike the blow.The heights are still beyond, but he is slowly rising, and day by day hope grows brighter. May God continue this progress until he shall stand shoulder to shoulder with the highest civilisation and culture of the world.

REV. DANIEL W. DAVIS

Africa is marching on. We need something more in keeping with the development of time. We need the development of something new. We need a present time ideological instrument effect to put us on the march. We need something to bring back that brotherly love, that patriotic feeling which is so badly lacking in Africa at the present time. We need the germination of a national spirit. Our leaders need new blood rejuvenation; let us help them to relight the fire, that fire which burnt so fiercely and vigorously during the precolonial era; let us help them, let us support them through the spirit of national agrarianism.

DR. ABRAHAM JEROME

We want to create conditions such that in this generation disease,hunger, poverty, illiteracy and ignorance should begin to vanish for ever from our society.

SAMORA MOISES MACHEL

There will be periods, such as the present, when our progress will be slow, as a result there will be bitterness and frustration. But I see a sign of hope. Our task must now be to transform these myths into reality of a political strategy and a social programme so that we can get on with the job of transforming Africa.

BAYARD RUSTIN

Steadily and firmly we are building up a better and richer life for our people and our continent. The liberation flame, although feeble and glimmering, still grows brighter each day. And the time is approaching when a new civilisation, a new culture, shall spring up from among our people, and the Nile shall once again flow through the land of science, of art and of literature, wherein will live Black Men of the highest accomplishments.

KWAME NKRUMAH

The most difficult problem of our times is how to think, so that the black race may regain its lost Paradise. We cannot apprehend and intelligently grasp, the things that make for regeneration, unless we think for ourselves fearlessly and even aggresively. We must continue thinking-thinking of the days that are no more, thinking of and for the present, thinking of the unknown tomorrow.

W.E.B. DUBOIS

I believe that white men should be white, yellow
men should be yellow, and black men should be
black in the great panorama of races, until each
and every race by its own intitiative lifts itself
up to the common standard of humanity, as to
compel the respect and appreciation of all and so
make it possible for each one to stretch out the
hand of welcome without being able to be
prejudiced against the other because of any
inferior and unfortunate condition.

MARCUS GARVEY

The great problem confronting this and future
generations is and will be how to bring about
results that make for the upbuilding of sterling
character; how with the opportunities at our command to make the next fifty years of freedom and
the entire future life proportionately worthy of
honourable mention.

DR. J.W.E. BOWEN

The battle for humanity is not lost or losing. All
across the skies sit signs of promise. The SLAVE
is rising in his might, the yellow millions are
tasting liberty, the black Africans are writhing
towards the light,and everywhere the labourer,with
ballot in his hand, is voting open the gates of
opportunity and peace...We must not falter,we must
not shrink. Above are the everlasting stars.

W.E.B. DUBOIS

Whoever imposes oppression, however large or small
the number of victims, and however understandable
the feelings of fear or revenge which promote it
racial discrimination is the mother of war, and
suffering, and loss of freedom for everyone. For if
men cannot live as men they will at least die as
men.

JULIUS NYERERE

As long as black people anywhere continue to be
oppressed on the grounds of their colour, black
people everywhere will stand together in opposition to that oppression, in the future as in the
past.

JULIUS NYERERE

We are not anti-white. We do not hate the European
because he is white. We hate him because he is an
oppressor. And it is plain dishonesty to say I
hate oppression and not the man who wields it.

ROBERT SOBUKWE

We must accept that the limit of tyrants are prescribed by the endurance of those whom they oppress. Our situation is not a mistake on the part of the whites but a deliberate act, and no amount of moral lecturing will persuade the white man to correct the situation.

STEPHEN BIKO

For us the choice is not between dying in battle or living under domination. Death is inalienable for man. The real choice is between living and fighting for victory or lying down under exploitation, domination and oppression.

SAMORA MOISES MACHEL

To be free is to participate in a community of those who are victims of oppression. Man is free when he belongs to a free community seeking to emancipate itself from oppression.

JAMES H. CONE

The time has passed when they could rule the country as if we, the people, did not exist. The time is against them, the world is against them. We on the other hand are encouraged by the great spirit of the people of South Africa,by the growth of the national liberatory movement, by the unprecedented political consciousness of the people and by the fact that the truth is with us. We enjoy the confidence of the whole world in this noble and just task for which we are pledged to fight until the dawn of freedom.

WALTER SISULU

We are fighting in order that in Africa there may exist a government chosen by the people, representing the will of the people and working for the good of the people of Africa. We fight so that we may destroy colonialism in every one of its forms.

AQUINO DE BRAGANCA

While the white liberal identifies with the blacks, the burden of the enormous privileges which he still uses and enjoys becomes lighter. Yet at the back of his mind is a constant reminder that he is quite comfortable as things stand and therefore should not bother about change.

STEPHEN BIKO

We can no longer come to terms with a situation where throughout the world all races should be free except the black race; where everything white is good and everything black is bad; where everything white is civilised and everything black is uncivilised. And that is precisely what the struggle is about, and that is why we must unite to change this state of affairs.

MOBUTU SEKO

Power concedes nothing without demand. It never did and never will find out just what any people will quietly submit to and you have found out the exact measure of injustice and wrong which will be imposed upon them, and these will continue till they are resisted with either words or blow, or with both. The limits of tyrants are prescribed by the endurance of those whom they oppress.

FREDERICK DOUGLAS

The struggle of the black people is part of this universal struggle for equality and human dignity. We cannot survive a free nation if there is any part of the world in which people of Africa colour or descent are treated as subhumans. We seek to affirm our rights and place not just in Africa but in the bigger village called the world.

TOM MBOYA

A man's colour, if it is black, is most frequently used as a means of enforcing economic limitations. It is used as a visible tool of oppression.

FLOYD B. MCKISSICK

The Negro has been starving not in the wilderness but in the midst of the worlds richest nations in the period of its greatest prosperity in history. He has been sighted, but whether his true condition has been diagnosed accurately and will be corrected by the majority is yet to be seen.

WHITNEY M. YOUNG. JNR

We must become convinced that colonialism is incapable of producing for the colonised peoples the material conditions which might make them forget their concern for dignity.

SEKOU TOURE

Politically, the white man dominates the African; economically,he exploits him;socially, he degrades his human status. It is these things that the African hates, and not the white man himself.

BASIL DAVIDSON

We are oppressed because we are black.We must use that very concept to unite ourselves and respond as a cohesive group.

STEPHEN BIKO

The dignity and beauty of man rests in the human spirit which makes him more than simply a physical being. This spirit must never be suppressed for exploitation by others. As long as the people recognise the beauty of their human spirits and move against suppression and exploitation.They will be carrying out one of the most beautiful ideas of all time. Because the human whole is much greater than the sum of its parts, the ideas will always be among the people. The prison cannot be victorious because walls, bars and guards cannot conquer or hold down an idea.

HUEY P. NEWTON

What we are, in fact, trying to do is to resolve our problems and difficulties as we encounter them; and it is this that we must dedicate ourselves to. We are making this attempt as people who have been conditioned by events which go as far back as 100 years of colonialism.

JULIUS NYERERE

Political Independence is a fact for large areas of Africa and the Caribbean. Colonialism has begun its journey out of life and into the museums of history. We now have to recognise that an end to colonialism is not an end to oppression based solely on colour.

JULIUS NYERERE

A state of rich and powerful men in which minority derices and imposes its will,whether we understand or not, would be the continuation in a new form of the situation against which we are struggling. The question of people's power is the essential question in our revolution.

SAMORA MOISES MACHEL

We have allowed death to change its name from Southern rope to Nothern hope. Too many black youths have been victimised by pushing dope into their veins instead of hope into their brains.

REV. JESSE L. JACKSON

For the black people to adopt their methods of relieving our oppression is ludicrous. We blacks must respond in our own way, on our own terms, in a manner which fits our temperament. The definitions of ourselves, the roles we pursue, the goals we seek are our responsibility.

STOKELY CARMICHAEL

During my lifetime I have dedicated myself to this struggle of the African people. I have fought against white domination, and I have fought against black domination. I have cherished the ideals of a democratic and free society in which all persons live together in harmony and with equal opportunities. It is an ideal which I hope to live for and achieve. But if needs be, it is an ideal for which I am prepared to die.

NELSON MANDELA

Freedom is within our grasp. Let us no longer quake or doubt about our capacity to enter into rightful heritage. Let there be no mistake about our future. We are determined to discard the yoke of oppression. We shall be free. History is on our side.

NNAMDI AZIKIWE

The only constructive thing a black man can do is to organise blacks to destroy the system that oppresses black people. We must never permit anyone, white or black, to destroy with impunity the product of a single drop of the blood and sweat of our people.

H. RAP BROWN

We could not achieve the new South Africa overnight, but we could begin to build it.We have suffered enough. We have suffered rape, plunder and oppression. We seek no vengance. More than other continents, perhaps, and as much as any other nation on this continent, we need the ways of peace, the ways of industry, the ways of concord.

CHIEF ALBERT LUTHULI

Black people must see liberation from the dominance and control of white society. Nothing less than this liberation will allow black people to determine their own destinies.

ROY INNIS

The stakes are really very simple:if we fail to do this, we face continued subjection to a white society that has no intention of giving up willingly or easily its position of priority and authority. If we succeed, we will exercise control over lives, politically, economically and psychologically.

STOKELY CARMICHAEL

Slavery and coloniasation has given the black man some of the arts of civilised life;but it must be added, that, denying him the inalienable rights of manhood, denying him the right to the product of his labour, it has left him no noble incentive to labour at these arts.

MRS. JOSEPHINE YATES

And when we finally reach that stage in which we can look at exploitations, segregation, racism, apartheid in the same way that historians now regard the Hitler Era in Germany or any other evil period of the past, we shall then do naturally and without self-consciousness what the Joyces and Dostoevskys of the world have always done - write intimately and objectively about our own people in universal human terms.

ARTHUR P. DAVIS

The history of the human race has been a struggle for the removal of mental, moral and spiritual oppression, and we would have failed had we not made our contribution to the struggle.

ROBERT SOBUKWE

I know that things cannot go on as they are going on now, that the outrageous manner in which we are at present treated cannot always continue. It is bound to end sooner or later.

F. J. GRIMBLE

We believe in the equality of races. We believe in the freedom of the people of all races. We believe in cooperation. In this struggle of ours, in this struggle to redeem Africa, we are fighting not against race and colour and creed. We are fighting against a system - a system which degrades and exploits.

KWAME NKRUMAH

The white said he was saving the Black's soul and that he was imposing his kind of peace for a civilising mission, but the black soon was convinced the colonialist had come to save his own soul, to fill his own purse, to bring prestige to his own nation, and perhaps to find someone before whom he could pretend to be superior.

W. E. B. DUBOIS

THE SACRIFICES OF THE BLACK RACE

If the great battle of human right against colour prejudice is to be won, it must be won not in our day, but in the day of our children's children. Ours is the blood and dust of battle, theirs is the rewards of victory.

W.E.B. DUBOIS

Changes must come. Changes for the better, but not without sacrifice.Your sacrifice. My sacrifice. We face tremendous odds.We know that.But our unity, our determination, our sacrifice,our organisation are our weapons.We must succeed ! We will succeed!

WALTER SISULU

The white man need expect no more Negro blood shed on his behalf. The first dying that is to be done by the black mam in the future will be to make himself free.

MARCUS GARVEY

After the sacrifices made and the blood that has been shed we cannot permit new parasites to come and feed on our sweat and labour.

SAMORA MOISES MACHEL

We have to work hard to evolve new patterns, new
social customs, new attitudes to life, so that while
we seek the material, cultural and economic advancement of our country, while we raise our people's
standard of life, we shall not sacrifice their fundamental happiness.

KWAME NKRUMAH

There is no easy walk to freedom anywhere and many
of us will have to pass through the valley of the
shadow of death again and again before we reach
the mountain top of our desires.

NELSON MANDELA

During my lifetime I have dedicated myself to this
struggle of African people. I have fought against
white domination and black domination. I have cherished the ideal of a democratic and free society
in which all persons live together in harmony and
with equal opportunities. It is an ideal which I
hope to live for and to see realised. If needs be,
it is an ideal for which I am prepared to die.

WILTON NKWAYI

We believe that the blood of Africa must flow to
free Africa. Africa is the last continent the black
man has to fight for and if he gives up fighting
that will be the end of him.

JULIUS NYERERE

The only constructive thing a black man can do is to organise blacks to destroy the system that oppresses black people. We must never permit anyone, white or black, to destroy with impunity the product of a single drop of the blood and sweat of our people.

H. RAP BROWN

The blood, sweat, tears and suffering of black people are the foundations of the wealth and power of the United States of America. We were forced to build America, and if forced to, we will tear it down.

HUEY NEWTON

Christ died to make men free. I shall die to give courage and inspiration to my race.

MARCUS GARVEY

Let every true black man be occupied in the highest employment of which his nature is capable, and die with the consciousness that he has done his best for the black race.

MARCUS GARVEY

Every man or woman who dies for Africa - if it is necessary to die - adds to Africa a new element of salvation, and hastens the day of her redemption.

MARCUS GARVEY

We are winning the struggle for which we have sac-
rificed, but we must even be ready to die to be
free, if that is what is necessary.

MARTIN LUTHER KING, JNR

Let us reinforce our rank and file in the fight
for freedom, no longer suffering in silence and
whinning like a dog, but strike back with all the
force at our command,when we are struck,preferring
to suffer the consequences of pressing forwards
our claim to a legacy of freedom, than to surrender our legacy to despoilers and usurpers.

NNAMDI AZIKIWE

For us, for our people and for our land, the time
has come to put an end to indecisions and promises, to adopt definitive action. We have already
made too many sacrifices, but we are determined to
make more to recover our freedom and human
dignity, whatever the path to be followed.

AMILCAR CABRAL

The black people have got to survive or be
destroyed by the white people.For a black man to
survive against the white races undying sacrifice
must be his first instinct. And this sacrifice
will have to be the embodiment of every single
concept including bloodshed or death in this
struggle for survival.

W.E.B. DUBOIS

... a war that never concerned any black man in the world. It was your war; but when it was too much for you you called for help, and millions of us black men went from West Africa, from East Africa, from the West Indies, from the United States of America; and today the blood of our boys has soaked the soil, their bones are buried in flanders. Not for any political reason on behalf of the black man but an answer to save the world for democracy. That was the urge that called us into war. Two millions of us answered, and hundreds of thousands of us paid the price.

MARCUS GARVEY

THE BLACK RACE OBSTACLES

Shunted to the right and left, with our path continually obstructed, and our ambition jeered at, we have kept quietly and persistently on, until we can now show we are sufficiently powerful to be regarded as a force.

J. PORTER

A man's colour,if it black,is most frequently used as a means of enforcing economical limitations. It is used as a visible tool of oppression.

FLOYD B. MCKISSICK

Racism is man's gravest threat to man - the maximum of hatred for a minimum of reason.

ABRAHAM JOSHUA HESCHEL

If, as everyone admits, white racism has blocked black aspiration since the beginning of the century then only a political struggle to compel respect for the black experience can compel change. Education alone can solve nothing, for the ultimate question concerns the political content of the education.

MAGRCUS GARVEY

202

It is not native incapacity and the want of vital manhood that limit the black man's progress in civilisation, but it is the fight made against him on the ground of his previous condition. Remove this and give the black man the white man's chance and he will keep pace with the white man in his march toward civilisation.

BISHOP L.H. HOLSEY

If the black man does not discover the truth, his life will be forever veiled in mystery, not only to whites, but to himself; and he will be heir to all the world interpretations of his personality.

CHESTER HINES

Let the world take no backward step in that slow but sure progress which has successively refused to let the spirit of class, of privilege, or of birth, debar from life, liberty and the pursuit of hapiness a striving human soul.

W.E.B. DUBOIS

The way of preparations for action lies in our rooting out all impurity and indiscipline from our organisation and making it the bright and shining instrument that will cleave its way to Africa's freedom.

NELSON MANDELA

It is a question of the Third World starting a new history of Man, a history which will have regard to the sometimes prodigious theses which Europe has put forward, but which will also not forget Europe's crimes of which the most horrible was committed in the heart of man.

FRANTZ FANON

The road is long and full of difficulties.At times the route strays off course,and it is necessary to retreat; at times a too rapid force separates us from the masses, and on occasions the pace is slow and we feel upon our necks the breath of those who follow upon our heels.

CHE GUEVARA

Today,in spite of our military coups and cesspools of corruption and conflicting tribalism, our darkness recedes and in the lightening landscape we begin to see our people more clearly – a kindly and smiling people even under the burden of injustice and misfortune.

MOKWUGO OKOYE

The Negro has been starving not in the wilderness but in the midst of the world's richest nations in the period of its greatest prosperity in history. He has been sighted,but whether his true condition has been diagnosed accurately and will be corrected by the majority is yet to be seen.

WHITNEY M. YOUNG, JNR

We want peace, freedom and cooperation between men and between all peoples. But for this very reason and cause, we must put an end to colonialism in our land, we must remove all obstacles to our national independence, we are fighting and are going to eliminate all those who, with weapons in hand, seek, but certainly in vain to prevent the liberation of our people.

AMILCAR CABRAL

The Negro needs a nation and a country of his own where he can best show evidence of his own ability in the art of human progress. Scattered as an unmixed and unrecognised part of alien nations and civilisations is but to demonstrate his imbecility,and point him out as an unworthy derelict, fit neither for society of Greek, Jew, nor Gentile.

MARCUS GARVEY

Our struggle - our resistence- must be waged on all levels of the life of our people. We must destroy everything the enemy can use to continue their domination over our people, but at the same time we must be able to construct everything that is needed to create a new life in our land.

MARCUS GARVEY

The main difficulty of the race question does not lie so much in the actual condition of the blacks as it does in the mental attitude of the whites.

JAMES WELDON JOHNSON

We could not achieve the new South Africa overnight, but we could begin to build it. We have suffered enough. We have suffered rape, plunder and oppression. We seek no vengeance. More than other continents, perhaps, and as much as any other nation on this continent, we need the ways of peace, the ways of industry, the ways of concord.

CHIEF ALBERT LUTHULI

After years of struggle against almost insurmountable odds, under conditions but little removed from slavery itself, the black man asks a fair and just judgement, not of those whose prejudice has endeavoured to forestall - to frustrate - his every forward movement; rather those who have lent a helping hand that he might demonstarte the truth of " The fatherhood of God and the brotherhood of man ".

GEORGE WHITE

The right is ours and God's. Let contrary sentiment and cross opinions go to the winds. Opposition to race independence is the weapon of the
enemy to defeat the hopes of an unfortunate
people. We are entitled to our own opinions and
not obligated to or bound by the opinions of
others.

MARCUS GARVEY

A race in a day is a splendid record. But a race
that came out of the wilderness, constructed its
own cities, built its own roads, and in contest
with its nature and poverty, wrestled until it won
a new name. That nation with its scars, its
experiences, and its development has for more to
be desired, and has far more resources upon which
to draw in its after contests than the former.

J.R. PORTER

Africa today remains the only continent which
suffers from the slings and arrows of hostility,
segregation, apartheid and exploitation. Africa is
the only continent that has suffered the greatest
indignity ever recorded. Africa today is the only
continent that still bleeds, and events show that
it has not reached the end of its suffering.

MOBUTU SEKO

There is no defence or security for any of us except the highest intelligence and development of all. If anywhere these are efforts tending to curtail the fullest growth of the Negro, let these efforts be turned into stimulating, encouraging, and making him the most useful and intelligent citizen. Effort or means so invested will pay a thousand per cent interest. These efforts will be twice blessed " blessing him that gives and him that takes ".

BOOKER T. WASHINGTON

We face an enemy that is deep-rooted, an enemy entrenched and determined not to yield. Our march to freedom is long an ddifficult. But both within and beyond our borders, the prospects of victory grow bright.

DR ALEX EKWUEME

If the great battle of human right against colour prejudice is to be won, it must be won not in our day, but in the day of our children's children. Ours is the blood and dust of battle, theirs is the rewards of victory.

W.E.B DUBOIS

In the world today a mighty struggle is taking place. It is a struggle to conquer the reign of an evil monster called discrimination - a monster that has wandered through this land for well over one hundred years stripping millions of black people of their sense of dignity and robbing them of their birth right of freedom.

MARTIN LUTHER KING, JNR

No black man, let him be American, West Indian or African, shall be truly respected until the race as a whole has emancipated itself through self-achievement and progress from universal prejudices.

MARCUS GARVEY

It is a hopeful sign that the black man is beginning, with some degree of seriousness, to turn his eyes inwards, to study himself, and try to discover what are his possibilities, and what obstructions that lie in the way to his larger developments.

PROF. W.H. CROGMAN

If we - and I mean the relatively conscious whites and the relatively conscious blacks,who must, like lovers, insist on, or create the consciousness of others - do not falter in our duty now, we may be able,handful that we are, to end the racial nightmare of our country and change the history of the world.

JAMES BALDWIN

Being black is a beautiful experience. It is the same way of living in an insane enviroment.

JAMES H. CONE

We are oppressed because we are black. We must use that very concept to unite ourselves and respond as a cohesive group.

STEPHEN BIKO

To like an individual because he's black is just as insulting as to dislike him because he isn't white.

E. CUMMINGS

Nationalism in Africa today is primarily a claim for equality of status and of rights, for personal dignity, self-respect, full participation in the things of the material world as well as in the things of the spirit: a consistent effort to rescue Africans from their condition of acquired inferiority to which they have been relegated through the years.

BASIL DAVIDSON

Let us turn our faces away from all the horrors of slavery, reconstruction and all kindred wrongs which have been heaped upon us, and stand up measuring the full statue of our American citizen, upon threshold of the new century as a New Man.

GEORGE H. WHITE

To be born in a free society and not be born free
is to be born into a lie.To be told by co-citizens
and co-Christians that you have no value, no
history, have never done anything that is worthy
of human respect destroys you because in the
beginning you believe it. Many negroes die because
they believe it.

JAMES BALDWIN

Mild demands and hypocritical smiles mislead white
America into thinking that all is fine and
peaceful. They mislead white America into thinking
that the path and pace chosen to deal with racial
problems are acceptable to masses of black
Americans. It is far better to speak forcefully
and truthfully. Only when one's true self - white
or black - is exposed, can this society proceed to
deal with the problems from a position of clarity
and not from one of misunderstanding.

STOKELY CARMICHAEL

Our surge to revolutionary reforms is late. If it
is so - if we are late in joining the modern age
of social enlightenement, late on gaining self-
rule, independence and democracy,it is because in
the past the pace has not been set by us.

CHIEF ALBERT LUTHULI

The conditions under which we work and live are changing. Promising prospects are opening up before us. We are on the verge of a new nation; a new horizon opens before all of us as a people and we are determined never to fail.

JULIUS NYERERE

MISCELLANEOUS QUOTATIONS

History is a process, not progress, and the idea and techniques of each age are products and parts of that process and cannot stand outside it. Yet, a bird we hold in hand in the present is worth more than twenty in the past or future and if we do not command success in all we hope for, it is enough if we conduct ourselves well enough to deserve success and leave the rest to fortune.

MOKWUGO OKOYE

The world wants more joy; the world cries for more sunshine; the world begs for a laugh. Mankind gloats over the depiction of deeds both noble and ignoble. The world delights in that which is novel. The Black Man is a son caloric. His presence is sunshine. He tells himself a novelty, and it will not be too far in the twentieth century before he will take pity on the world and mankind and write them what they like.

WALTER L. LEWIS

A civilisation that chooses to close its eyes to its crucial problems is a stricken civilisation.

AIME CESAIRE

The history of man through the ages shows that his path has its ups and downs but that the traveller marches wearily on, making use of any short cuts or detours as the need or opportunity arises.

MOKWUGO OKOYE

I want to be the white man'sbrother, not his brother-in-law.

MARTIN LUTHER KING,JNR

The ultimate weakness of violence is that it is a descending spirit begetting the very thing it seeks to destroy.
Instead of diminishing evil, it multiplies it. Through violence you may murder liars, but you cannot murder th lie, nor establish the truth.

MARTIN LUTHER KING, JNR

The past has shown the role of the unexpected, of what was not and could have been anticipated, but which having occurred, takes its place as part of the possible order of things.

MOKWUGO OKOYE

Perfection may be beyond our reach, but we must forever strive to extend our grasp - for what else is heaven for ?

MOKWUGO OKOYE

What our forefathers searched for and looked
forward anxiously to see, what all of them
strongly desired, what they missed terribly, has
now been made possible and we of this generation
now have it before us to behold as a living
reality.

WILLIAM OFORI ATTA

There are those who take the view that reality
depends on the way in which man interprets it. For
such reality are the consequences of what man has
in his head.
There are others who take the view that reality
exists and that man forms part of reality. It is
not what he has in his head that defines reality,
but reality itself defines man. Man is part of
reality,man is within reality and it is not what
he has in his head that defines reality. Reality
itself under which the man lives is what defines
the things man has in his head.

AMILCAR CABRAL

Growth and change more often than not produce
tensions as the old gives way to the new in
fulfilment of nature's purposes.

MOKWUGO OKOYE

The Black Man is ignored today simply because he has kept himself backward; but if he were to try to raise himself to a higher state in the civilised cosmos, all the other races would be glad to meet him on the plane of equality and comradeship. It is indeed unfair to demand equality when one of himself has done nothing to esatblish the right to equality.

JOHN HENRIK CLARKE

Being subservient to the will and caprice of progressive races will not prove anything superior in us. Being satisfied to drink of the dregs from the cup of human progress will not demonstrate our fitness as a people to exist along side of others, but when of our own initiative we strike out to build industries, government and ultimately, empires,then and only then will we as a race,prove to our Creators, and to man in general, that we are fit to survive and capable of shaping our own destiny.

MARCUS GARVEY

'...Africa is not an extension of any other continent....It devolves on us to establish our own African Community, geographically prescribed. That is why I consider that the step which we have taken is so important a step towards the establishment of this African Community, which will have its own distinctive outlook - an African Personality.

KWAME NKRUMAH

The mists of nationalist euphoria, the smokescreen of charismatic demagogy, the fogs of Cold War propaganda - all these have felt the useful blow and blast of many gales of argument and action.

BASIL DAVIDSON

When I search for Man in the technique and the style of Europe, I see a succession of negations of man, and and avalanche of murders.

FRANTZ FANON

Let us not imitate Europe by creating states, institutions and societies which draw their inspiration from her. Humanity is waiting for something other from us than such an imitation, which would be almost an obscene caricature.

FRANTZ FANON

The race question is subsidiary to the class question in politics, and to think of imperialism in trems of race is disastrous. But to neglect the racial factor as merely incidental is an error only less grave than to make it fundamental.

C.L.R. JAMES

Hope may be a fraud, an illusion helping us to endure life or the bait by which nature gets her in our nose. If hopes are dupes fears may be liars.

MOKWUGO OKOYE

Returning violence for violence multiply violence, adding deeper darkness to a night already devoid of stars. Darkness cannot drive out darkness, only light can do that. Hate cannot drive out hate,only love can do that.

MARTIN LUTHER KING, JNR

Man, in spite of his innumerable failings and series of disaster that have trailed his uneven progress, has hurled defiance at the elemental powers, and with his mind, cradle of evolution, sought to master them, paying untold sacrifices and all he held dear for truth, for faith, for freedom, for justice, for honour and country - a quality for which much may be forgiven him and for which it is impossible to lose hopes for him.

MOWUGO OKOYE

There is apparently no limit to the capacity of man to penetrate the secrets of nature and the universe, and as part of the marvel of existence, which in its unity has many manifestations, man has the gift of seeing and comprehending the nature and meaning of the universe through observation and contemplation,experiment and deduction.

MOKWUGO OKOYE

There is light to which we cannot climb by using
the active intelligence of our own minds. Mind
creates, and as much as we desire in Nature we can
have through the creation of our own minds.

MARCUS GARVEY

We are not only men linked to Africa by birth and
history. We are also citizens of our own nations;
we are also Christians, or Moslims, socialists, con-
servatives or communists.
These are more truly a reflection of ourselves
than is our colour or ancestry.

JULIUS NYERERE

So, while, in Tennyson's words, we are "ever
reaping something new" and what we "have done but
earnest of the things that we shall do", we can
hope that we, as part of the gigantic reality that
is the process of evolution, will continue to rise
from lower to higher forms of living and that each
tomorrow shall bring us farther than today.

MOKWUGO OKOYE

The Third world today faces Europe like a collosal
man whose aim should be to try to resolve the
problems to which Europe has not been able to find
answers.

FRANTZ FANON

I would be untrue to the faith of my fathers, untrue to my conscience, untrue to my God, if I did not stand on a platform of racial righteousness, racial truth, racial honour and racial self-respect.

MARCUS GARVEY

The white man does not yet know the Black Man. The white man does not know him after many years of contact. To know the Black Man one must be with him and become a part of his life - see what he is doing, and above all, to know what he is thinking.

PROF. WILLIAM SCARBOROUGH

Who are the components of the 'the whole' ? If you destroy all the individuals by taking away their rights, for whom do you keep the interests of society as a whole ? The idea that society is an end in itself must have caused the French King to ask, 'The State ? Who is the State ? I am the State !'

DR. J.B. DANQUAH

I am a student of the universe and never really the master. Once you think you can't lose an argument, once you think you can't be corrected, then you are a fool.

HUEY P. NEWTON

We do not want to catch up with anyone. What we want to do is to go forward all the time, night and day, in the company of man, in the company of all men.

FRANTZ FANON

History is not pleasant, but we must make it so. We must labour and seek to find our sufficiently beauty, to serve it, win it, and increase it, counting even death as nothing so long as the dying eyes still turn to it.

MOKWUGO OKOYE

Nkrumah fought the good fight and now belongs to the ages. We can do worse than follow in his footsteps and, benefitting from his experience, make our live sublime so that departing, we may leave behind us footprints on the sands of Time.

MOKWUGO OKOYE

When there is violence there is messiness. Violence brings too many residues of hate into the reconstruction period. Apart from its obvious horrors, it creates too many post-revolutionary problems. If at all possible, we want the revolution to be peaceful and reconciliatory.

STEPHEN BIKO

Every now and then the world needs a David to stand up to a Goliath ; power needs to be challenged.

SEKOU TOURE

Be the truth what it may, I shall seek it on the pure assumption that it is worth seeking - and Heaven nor Hell, God nor the Devil shall turn me from my purpose till I die.

W.E.B. DUBOIS

Education is a medium by which a people are prepared for the creation of their own particular civilisation, and the advancement and glory of their own race.

MARCUS GARVEY

We must become convinced that colonialism is incapable of producing for the colonised peoples the material conditions which might make them forget their concern for dignity.

SEKOU TOURE

If we want to turn Africa into a new Europe and America into a new Europe, then let us leave the destiny of our countries to Europeans. They will know how to do it better than the most gifted among us.

FRANTZ FANON

But if we want humanity to advance a step further,
if we want to bring it up to a diffrent level than
that which Europe has shown it, then we must invent
and we must make discoveries.

FRANTZ FANON

STATEMENTS BY BLACK ORGANISATIONS

We must be sheep to our friends but vicious to our enemies wherever we are, if we really wish to win back our freedom and country. The basic aim of every worker in Zimbabwe today must be how best to destroy the enemy's means of livelihood because it is on this he depends for power. An exploiter without means of production is as helpless as a fish out of water. The worker and peasant is the basis for success.

A STATEMENT BY ZAPU

The freedom of the African people, the elimination of the exploitation of man by man and the restitution of democracy, liberty and harmony in South Africa are such vital and fundmental matters that the government and the Public must know that we all fully resolved to achieve them in our lifetime.

A STATEMENT BY AFRICAN NATIONAL CONGRESS

As a defenceless and voteless people, we have explored other channels without success.The African people are left with no alternative but to embark upon the campaign to redouble our efforts for the attainment of citizenship rights.

A STATEMENT BY AFRICAN NATIONAL CONGRESS

Revolution liberates man. It liberates his intelligence and his work. This liberation manifests itself in the development of our production, which serves the people, which serves the struggle. To produce is to learn,learn in order to produce and struggle better.

A STATEMENT OF FRELIMO(MOZAMBIQUE)

Our peoples and the colonists have differnt destinies which we shall fulfil in peace, amity, cooperation and equality of rights and duties. We are Africans and it is to Africa that our destinies have been and always will be linked.

A STATEMENT BY FRELIMO

No, we have all had enough of so much oppression. The torture is coming to an end. It is time to demand our rights. But if the colonialists do not wish to leave, what are we going to do ? ONLY FIGHT. It is only through struggle that they will be convinced we want freedom, that we want to take back our land.

A STATEMENT BY FRELIMO

Africa is only for Africans and we do not accept the intervention of any outsider. Many promise us their assistence but it is we who must take the initiative. We are going to expel them !

A STATEMENT BY <u>FRELIMO</u>

We are not fighting to become Portuguese with black skins. We are fighting to affirm ourselves as Mozambicans, whithout this meaning contempt for the Portuguese people or any other people. In this respect, FRELIMO reaffirms its wish to fully cooperate with all peoples in the world on a basis of independence, equality, respect and mutual interest.

A STATEMENT BY <u>FRELIMO</u>

BIOGRAPHIES OF AUTHORS

ABBOUD, JUMBA

He was born in 1900 in Sudan. He joined the army
and rose to Commander-in-Chief of the independent
Sudan in 1956. He became a political leader and
assumed control of the country in 1958. In 1964 he
was removed from the presidency in a bloodless
revolution.

AGGREY, DR JAMES KWEGGIR

He was born in 1875 in the Gold Coast, now Ghana.
He was a christian educationalist who went to the
U.S.A to study in 1898. He graduated with B.A. in
1902 at Livingstone College. He became noted as an
interpreter of Africa to western audiences. He
died in 1927 in New York.

ANDRIAMANTATO, RICHARD

He was born in Madagascar and educated at
University of Strasborg in 1957. He gained a
degree in Theology and Philosophy and returned
home in the same year
He was elected Major of Tananarive in 1959 and to
the National assembly for Tananarive in 1960. He
served in the army and was appointed Colonel and
rose to be Brigadier-General in 1971.He became a
member of the Cabinet.

ARMATTOE, DR R.A.

He was born in the Volta Region, Gold Coast, now known as Ghana. He studied medicine in England and became a scientist. He could speak English,German, and French. He once said,"No university can confer a degree on me". He thought he was too brilliant to be above a degree.He wrote "Deep down the black man's mind". He died at the age of 39.

AQUINO de BRAGANCO, PROF

He is a Mozambican scholar who has been involved for over 20 years in the struggle of African people to rid themselves of Portuguese rule.He now heads the Centre for African Studies at Eduardo Mondlane University in Maputo.

AZIKIWE, DR NNAMDI

He was born in Nigeria in 1904. He studied at Howard University and Lincoln University and returned home to found "West African Pilot" in 1937. He became the first president of Nigeria, 1963-1966. He is regarded the father of modern Nigerian Nationalism.He is a journalist,an author, a politician and a businessman.

BALDWIN, JAMES

He was born in 1924 in New York.For a short period he followed his father's footsteps by becoming a preacher. He was one of the black profilic and celebrated writers.

He had fourteen books to his credit and held many literary honours.

BALEWA, ALHAJI SIR ABUBAKAR

He was born in Northern Nigeria in 1912. He became the first Prime Minister of Nigeria. He was assassinated in a military coup in 1966.

BIBB, PROF JOSEPH D

He was born in Montogemery, Alabama, where he received his primary education. He enetered Fisk University and Livingstone College,N.C, where he studied Law and theology. He spent two years as Professor of Hebrew and Bible History at Morris Brown College.

STEPHEN BIKO

He was born in Cape Province of South Africa in 1946. He went to Natal University to study medicine in 1966.
He was elected in 1968 the first president of the all-black South African Student Organinisation. From then on he engaged himself in various political activities which resulted in his arrest on many occasions.
In 1977 he was arrested, tried and detained. In the same year he died in police custody. The actual cause of his death still remains unresolved.

BLYDEN, EDWARD WILMOT

He was born in the West Indies. He went to the United States of America for theological training. He emigrated to Liberia in 1850 and died in 1912 in Siera Leone.

BOUMEDIENNE, HOUARI

He was born in 1927 in Algeria. In 1962 he was appointed Minister of National Defence in Ben Bella's first cabinet. In 1963 he was named First Deputy Premier. He seized power in a bloodless coup in 1965.

BOWEN, REV. J.W.E.

He was born in 1861 in New Orleans. After his university education at New Orleans University he was appointed Professor of Classics.He later joined the Methodist as a pastor. He was a voluminous writer; his publications include "The American and the African Negro".

BOWSER, MRS ROSA D.

She was born in Virginia,U.S.A., and brought up in the city of Richmond.
She worked as an educator in which capacity she was able to found the Women's League which rendered signal service in the Lunemburg trials.
She was president of Richmond Mothers' Club, a member of the executive Board of the Southern Federation of Coloured Women, chairman of the

Standing Committee of Domestic Economy for the Hampton conference.

BROWN, H, RAP

He was born in Louisiana,U.S.A. He graduated at Southern University. He took a position at Howard University. He became involved in the Black Movement in 1960. In 1966-67 he worked in Alabama as SNCC representaive. He succeeded Stokely Carmichael as chairman of SNCC in 1967.

CABRAL, AMILCAR

He was born in 1924 in Portuguese Guinea, West Africa. He became the Secretary-General of the African Party. He was assassinated in 1973 by Portuguese agents.

STOKELY CARMICHAEL

He was born in Port-of-Spain,Trinidad.
He received much of his education in New York City and Washington,D.C.
He graduated from Howard University.
He has a long history of active participation in the Black Movement, and helped found Lowndes County Freedom organisation in Alabama.
He was elected chairman of SNCC, but later broke away to become a member of the Black Panter Party.

231

CESAIRE, AIME

He was born in 1913 in Martinique. He studied in France in 1931, and returned home to teach. He was elected Deputy to the French National Assembly for Martinique. He became mayor of Fort de France.

CHISHOLM, SHIRLEY

She was born in Brooklyn in 1924. She is the first Black woman to be elected to Congress. She has two honorary degrees: Doctor of Humane o fLetter and Doctor of Laws.

CHITEPO, HERBERT

He was born in 1923 in Zimbabwe, then Rhodesia. He was Rhodesia's first African barrister.He was el- ected director of ZANU.He went into exile in 1962, and became Tanganyika's first African Director of Public Prosecution.

CLARKE, JOHN HENRIK

He was born in 1915 in Union Springs, Alabama. He went to New York to pursue a career as a writer in 1933. He attended New York University and majored in history and world literature. He has published over fifty short stories.
He was Associate Professor in the Department of Black and Puerto Rican Studies at Hunter College, New York City, and a distinguished Visiting Professor of African History at Africana Studies

and Research Centre at Cornell University.He was co-founder and associate editor of the Harlem Quarterly (1949-1950).

CLEAVER, ELDRIDGE

He was born in 1935 in Wabbasaka, Arkansas. He is the author of many essays on the Black Panther ideology. He became a senior editor of Rampart Magazine. He is a political exile in Algeria.

CANE, JAMES H.

He was born in 1938 in Fordyce, Arkansas. He is a theologian, educator and author. He is the author of "Black Theology and Black Power", "A Black Theology of Liberation". He is a member of Ecumenical Association of Third World Theologians.

COUNCILL, PROF. W.H.

He was born in Fayetteville, North Carolina,1848. He left Alabama in 1857 where he became enrolling clerk of the Alabama House of Representatives.
He was appointed President Grant Receiver of the Land Office for Northern District of Alabama in 1875.
He was admitted to the Supreme Court of Alabama in 1883.
He founded and edited "Huntsville Herald", and co-edited "The Lamp Wisdom".

COX, REV. J.M.

He was born in Alabama in 1860. He entered Clark University to study classics, and then went on to study theology in 1886. He was appointed lecturer of ancient languages in Philander Smith College, Arkansas. After eleven years he was appointed President of the institution.

CROGMAN, PROF. W.H.

He was born on the island of St. Martin in 1841. In 1855 he went to the U.S.A. to study Greek and Latin in Clark University,Atlanta. After completing his academic course he was appointed a Professor of Classics in 1880. He wrote "Talks for the Times","The Negro's Claims" and "The Negro's Need".

CULP, DR. D.W.

He was born in 1854 in South Carolina. He graduated from Biddle university in Classics and from Princeton Theological Seminary in History of Philosophy and Psychology.
In 1881 he was elected Principal of Stanton Institute.

DANQUAH, DR. J.B.

He was born in 1895 in Ghana. He was a well-known politician and barrister, popularly known as the Doyen of Ghana politics. He was one of the six Gold Coast politicians detained by the British Government after the 1948 riots. He was detained by Nkrumah and died in 1965 in prison.

DAVIS, REV. DANIEL WEBSTER

He was born in 1862 in Richmond, U.S.A. After his public education in 1878 he started teaching. In 1895 he was ordained to the Ministry and attached to the Baptist Church of Manchester. His book "Ideal Moments" established him as a poet.

DOUGLAS, FREDERICK

He was born in 1818 in Maryland, U.S.A. He escaped from his master to New York and then to Massachusetts.
He practised oratory with the aim of speaking against the evils of slavery.
One of his greatest speeches was his 4th of July speech at Rochester,1852, in which he indicted every power structure in American life.
The city of Rochester erected a monument to his memory. He died in 1895.

DUBOIS, W.E.B.

He was born in Great Barrington, Massachusetts in 1869. He entered Fisk University in 1885 and graduated in 1888. He was the founder of Niagara Movement, the NAACP and the Pan-African Movement. He was the bridge between the militant Frederick Douglas and the current Movement for racial Justice and Equality. He died in Accra, Ghana, in 1963 at the age of 95.

FRANTZ FANON

He was born in 1925 in Martinique. He studied medicine in France and later specialised in psychiatry. He was assigned to a hospital in Algeria during the rising against the French. He died in 1961 of leukaemia in Washington D.C. at the age of 36.

FARMER, JAMES L.

He was born in 1920 in Marshall, Texas. He took degrees at Wiley College in 1938 and Howard University in 1941. He was the founder of Congress of Racial Equality. He was appointed National Director of CORE. He ran against Shirley Chisholm for United States Representative in Congress for New York's twelfth district.

FORTUNE, THIMOTY THOMAS

He was born in Florida in 1856. in 1876 he entered Howard University. His career as a journalist began in 1880 when he began publication of "New York Globe" and "New York Freeman". He was the first president of the Afro-American League. He was elected chairman of the National Afro-American Press Association, chairman of National Negro Business League. He was a Republican in politics. In the presidential election of 1900 he took an active part in the political canvass of that year, advocating the re-election of President McKinley.

GARVEY, MARCUS

He was born in 1887 in Jamaica. He formed Univeral Negro Improvement Association (UNIA) to alert the black people all over the world to their potential and their heritage. He established a weekly paper "The Negro world". He attracted hostility by his statement,"Back to Africa". He was deported from U.S.A. in 1927, and in 1940 died in London.

GRIMBLE, FRANCIS J.

He was born in South Carolina in 1850. He entered Lincoln University and graduated in 1870. He also held a degree from Princeton Theological Seminary,

1878. He wrote the book,"The Negro:The Forces for and against Him".

HARLLEE, PROF. N.W.

He was born in Robeson County, North Carolina. He graduated at Biddle University in 1879, and served as Principal of a grammar school,Dallas,Texas. He also served as president and as secretary of the Teachers' State Association of the State of Texas. He was the author of "Simplified Long Division", a new graphic method of teaching long division.

HAWKINS, PROF. JOHN RUSSELL

He was born in Warren County, North Narolina, in 1862. After his graduation in 1881 went to Hampton Institute where he spend a year studying business. He was an ardent advocate of higher education for the Negro. In 1896 he was appointed by the General conference of the African Methodist Episcopal as Commissioner of Education.

HEARD, DR. WILLIAM H.

He was born in 1850 in Elbert County, Georgia, U.S.A. He attended South Carolina University, Clark University and Atlanta University. He was elected to South Carolina Legislature from Abbeville County in 1876.He was appointed Minister Resident and Consul General to Liberia by President Grover in 1895.

HEWIN, J. THOMAS

He was born in 1871 in Dinisiddie County, Va, U.S.A. He graduated from Boston University Law School and was admitted to the Bar. He organised the Anti-Deadly weapon league among the young blacks. He was an orator of Frederick Douglas type.

HOLSEY, BISHOP L.H.

Born near Columbus, Ga,in 1842,U.S.A. In 1868 he was licensed to preach in the M.E. Church and served the Hancock Circuit. In 1870 he was elected a delegate to the first General Conference of the Coloured Methodist Episcopal Church held in America. He was the founder of Paine College in Augusta,Ga.

INNIS, ROY

He was born in 1934 at St. Crox, Virgin Islands. He moved to the U.S.A. with his family and settled in Harlem. He is an outspoken man and a principal advocate of neo-black nationalism. He was elected in 1965 as chairman of the Harlem Chapter of CORE until 1968 when he was elected national assocaite director.

JACKSON, REV. JESSE L.

He was born in 1941 in Greenville, South Carolina. He earned his Bsc. in sociology in 1964. He received DD degree from Lincoln University.

He was one of Martin Luther King's, Jnr. top aides. He contested the Democratic Party nomination for the Presidency in 1984 and in 1988.

JOHNSON, PROF. J. WELDON

He was born in Jacksonville,Fla,U.S.A. He graduated from Atlanta University. He was the editor of the "Daily American ", an afternoon paper. In 1898 he was admitted to the Bar and to the Supreme Court of Florida. He wrote the words, "Lift Every Voice and Sing", a national hymn for the coloured people of America.

JONES, LEROI

He was born in 1934 in Newark, New Jersey, U.S.A. He studied at Howard University, Colombia University and the New School of Social Research in New York.He began his career as an avant-garde writer. He was awarded the Whitney Fellowship in 1961-62, and a Guggenheim Award in 1964-65.He is the founder of the Black Arts Repertory Theatre in Harlem.

KENYATTA, JOMO

He was born into Kikuyu tribe in 1891 in Kenya. He studied for his degree in London in 1931. In 1945, with George Padmore and Kwame Nkrumah he formed the Pan African Federation and helped organised the Fifth Pan African congress in Manchester.

In 1946 he returned home to lead the Kenya African Union. In 1952 he was arrested and imprisoned for his involvement in the Mau Mau activities. He became the first President of Kenya.

KERR, REV. S

He graduated from Rawden College, Leeds, England and returned to the West Indies. In 1859 he did extensive missionary work in the Turks and Caicos Islands.In 1873 he was appointed professor in the National Lyceum College.In 1880 he was advanced to the Priesthood of the Episcopal Church of America. In 1889 he made an extensive missionary tour through Central America,where he performed religious services at the opening of the Nicaragua Canal. In 1890 he returned to the West Indies and was transferred to the Dioscese of Florida and made Rector of St. Peter's Episcopal Church in the Key West.

KING, MARTIN LUTHER, JNR.

He was born in Atlanta in 1929. He was awarded PhD in systematic Theology from Boston University. He was the ordained pastor at Ebenezer Baptist Church in Atlanta.
He was awarded the Nobel Peace Prize for his efforts on behalf of peace and mankind in general in 1964.
He was the undisputed leader of the non-violent faction of the Civil rights movement.
He was shot dead in Memphis,Tennessee on April 4, 1968.

KNOX, GEORGE L.

He was born in 1841 in Wilson County, Tenna., U.S.A.
In 1862 he joined the union forces in the civil
war. He took active part in politics as a repub-
lican and in 1896 was elected a delegate to the
National Convention in Minneapolis when President
McKinley was nominated.

LEWIS, WALTER L.

He was born in South Carolina, U.S.A. He graduated
at Briddle University and took up a teaching job.
He moved to Florida in 1890. He was appointed editor of the labour Union Recorder, and in 1896 went
to Jacksonville as a reporter for the "Metropolis".

LUMUMBA, PATRICE

He was born in the Congo now called Zaire in 1925.
Inspired by the meeting of fellow Africans in
Ghana, he formed a political party, The Movement
National Congolese. He became the first Prime
Minister in 1960, and was killed by his enemies,
who tortured him. In Moscow there is a University
called Lumumba.

LUTHULI, CHIEF ALBERT JOHN

He was born in 1898 in South Africa. He became in
1936 a local chief of his tribe.
He was appointed President of African National

Congress in 1951 and President-General the same year. His greatness was acknowledged by the award of the Nobel Peace Prize. He died in 1967.

MACHEL,SAMORA MOISES

He was born in 1933 in Mozambique. In 1970 he was elected President of the country. He died in a plane crash in 1986. His death was attributed to the South Africa Government.

MALCOLM X

He was born in 1925 in Omaha, Nebraska, as Malcolm Little. He became acquainted with the Black Muslim Sect and later became its most advocate. He left it to form the Organisation of Afro-American Unity. He was assassinated in 1965.

MANDELA, MRS WINNIE

She was born in 1934 in Transkei, South Africa. She became the first black woman medical worker in South Africa. She married Nelson Mandela in 1958. Since 1958 she has been imprisoned time and again and since 1962 has been under house arrest.

MANDELA, NELSON

He was born in 1918 in Transkei, South Africa. He holds a degree of Bachelor of Arts from the University of South Africa and is a qualified solicitor. His association with Walter Sisulu aroused his political interest.

In 1944 he joined the African National congress and was elected General Secretary. His political activities brought him face to face with the government on many occasions. In 1963 he was arrested, tried and imprisoned. Despite international pressure for his release, Mandela remains in prison to this day.

MARABLE, MANNING

He is Professor of Political Sociology and a Director of the Africana and Hispanic Studies Programme at Colgate University, New York. He is the author of How Capitalism Underdeveloped Black America.
He is a regular contributor to Black Scholar, The Nation and The New Statesman.

MASON, REV. M.C.B

He was born in 1859 near Houma,La,U.S.A. He entered the Gammon Theological Seminary at Atlanta,Ga., graduating therefrom in 1891. He got his Doctor of Philosophy from Syracuse University, N.Y. He was the first black man to be elected Field Agent of the Freedman's Aid Society of the Methodist Episcopal Church.

MAZRUI, ALI

He was born in 1933, Mombasa,Kenya. He was a
university Professor of Political Science from
1963 to 1965, Makerere University College, Uganda.
His appointment include: visiting professorial
scholar, University of Chicago,Harvard,Singapore.
His publications include: Protest and Power in
Black Africa, On Heress and Uhuru-Wishop and the
Anglo-African Commonwealth. He won the Wegner
Prize for Philosophy in 1958 and the Fleure Prize
for International Studies.

M'BA,LEON

He was born in 1902 at Libreville, Gabon. He
became Head of governement from 1957 to 1967. In
1964 there was a military coup but the French
military was called in, and he was reinstated.

MBOYA, TOM

He was born in 1930. He was a politician widely
regarded as the most likely successor to Jomo
Kenyatta as President. He was assassinated at the
age of 38.

MCKISSICK, FLOYD B.

He is a well-known constitutional lawyer who
handled civil rights cases. He received his degree
from North Carolina Law School. In 1966 he was appointed national director of CORE. He established
F.B. Mckissick Enterprises to promote black eco-

nomic development. For him black power is attainable through economic development.

MELADY, THOMASS P

He was born in 1921 in Norwich, Connecticut. He was the U.S.A. ambassador to Uganda and Urundi, senior advisor to U.S.A. delegation to the 25th U.N. General Assembly,1970.He founded the Institute of African affairs, Duquesne University in 1957. He was knighted by Pope Paul VI,1968,and Pope John Paul II, 1983.

MOBUTU, SEKO

He was born in 1930 in Zaire. He studied journalism,and worked for INFORCONCO in Brussels. He was a memeber of Lumumba's Movement Nationale Congolais. He was MNC delegate to the Round Table Conference in 1960 leading to independence. He became President of Zaire in 1965.

MUHAMMAD, ELIJAH

He was born in 1897 in Sandersville, Georgia, as Elijah Poole. He became Farad Muhammad's first minister of Islam and directed the Muslim training school. He founded Temple No. 2 in Chicago, presently the headquarters of the Muslim Movement. In 1942 he was jailed for encouraging resistance to the draft.

NEWTON, HUEY P.

He was born in Louisiana in 1942.
He was instrumental in founding the Black Panther
Party in 1965.
He is committed to a struggle for black self-
determination, and to political and economic
structure that meet the needs of the people.
He served a prison term for the alleged killing of
a white policeman. a decision which has since been
reversed.

NKRUMAH, KWAME

He was born in 1909 into Nzema tribe in Ghana. He
graduated from Lincoln University,U.S.A.,and
proceeded to London to continue his studies. In
1945, with George Padmore and Jomo Kenyatta he
formed the Pan African Federation and helped
organised the 5th Pan African Congress in Manchester. He was the founder of the modern Ghana
and became its first Prime Minister and President.
He was ousted in a military coup in 1966 while he
was visiting China. He was the moving spirit
behind the Charter of African States,1961. He died
in exile in Guinea in 1972.

NKWAYI, WILTON

He was born in 1923 in South Africa. He was a
leading member of the South Africa Congress of
Trade Union. Following on the Rivonia Trial he was
arrested and sentenced to life imprisonment on
Robben Island.

NUJOMA, SAM

He was born in Namibia. In 1959 he helped to form the Ovamboland People's Organisation (OPO). Later he helped to transform OPO into SWAPO of which he became president.

NYERERE, JULIUS

He was born in Butiana, Tanzania,in 1922. He was educated at Edinburgh University. He returned home to found Tanganyika African National Union (KANU). He was elected to the National Assembly in 1957 and became Prime Minister in 1961 and President in 1962. He retired from politics in 1985.

OBASANJO, GENERAL OLUSEGUN

He was born in 1933 in Nigeria. He was a military General who became Head of Federal Sate in 1976 in a bloodless coup. He is now retired and a prosperous farmer.

OFORI-ATTA, WILLIAM

He was born in Ghana in 1910. He qualified as a barrister in London. He was one of the Six Gold Coast politicians detained by the British Government after the 1948 riots. He became a cabinet minister in Nkrumah's government. He died in 1988.

OKOYE, MOWUGO

He is a Nigerian writer who has 25 books to his credit.He is a dabbler in abstract ideas covering politics, philosophy, religion, sociology and history. As a humanist his sympathy is wide and his commitment to social reform is strong.

PETTEY, MRS SARAH DUDLEY

She was born in New Berne, North Carolina. She entered the famous Seminary at Concord, North Carolina,from which she graduated in 1883.She read classics. Upon graduation she was appointed Vice Principal of New Berne school. For several years she was the Genral Secretary of the Women's Home and Foreign Missionary Society of the A.M.E. Zion Church.

PORTER, DR. J.R.

He was born and reared in Savannah,Ga.,U.S.A. He graduated in 1886 with B.A. He then entered Walden University,at that time Central Tennessee College, to study dentistry and qualified in 1889. He was the founder of Alabama Penny Savings Bank of Birmingham and the Secretary of its Board of directors. In the Birmingham strike of 1892/93 he moved to Atlanta and built up an excellent dental practice.

PURCELL, ISAAC LAWRENCE

He was born in Winnsboro, South Carolina.
He studied Law and was admitted to State Supreme Court of the U.S.A. in 1901. In politics he was a Republican, and for 12 years was the chairman of the Republican Executive Committee of Putnam. In 1895 he was elected a delegate to the Republican National Convention.

J.J.RAWLINGS

He was born and educated in Ghana. His father is a Scot and his mother a Ghananian. He was an officer in the Ghana Air Force. He staged two coups within three years. Since 1981 he has been the Head of State.

RICHARDSON PROF ARTHUR

He was born in 1863, St George's, Bermuda. He graduated from University of New Brunswick. He was appointed Principal of the Wilberforce Collegiate Institute of Chatham, Ontario. He emigrated to Atlanta to serve as the Principal of Morris Brown College. In 1898 he was offered the Presidency of Edward Waters College in Jacksonville, Fla.

RUSTIN, BAYARD

He was born in 1910 in Westchester, Pennsylvania.
He attended Wiberforce University in Ohio.
He became field secreatry for CORE.
He was the chief organiser of the 1963 Civil

Rights March on Washington. He was jailed as a concsientious objector during World War II.
For Rustin,the key to racial progress is not direct, violent action, but political action and social reform.

SCARBOROUGH, PROF. W.S.

He was born in 1852 in Macon, Ga.,U.S.A. In 1875 he graduated from Oberlin College, Ohio, in Philosophy and Classics.He was appointed Vice President of Wilberforce University, Ohio, and Professor of Greek and Latin in the same institution. He was elected President of the Afro-American State League to further the interests of the Negro in the country.

SEALE, BOBBY

He was born in 1894 in Brunswick, New York. He was a clergyman by profession, General Secretary of Greater New York Federation of Churches, 1934-38, editor of the Protestant World, 1950-53, Director of Community Relations Protestant Council of the City of new York, 1948-50. He died in 1967.

SENGHOR, LEOPOLD

He was born in 1906 in Senegal. He studied in Paris where he obtained his degree. He became a member of the Constituent assemblies of 1945. He

251

helped to draft the Constitution of the Fourth Republic. He represented Senegal in the French National Assembly. He became President in 1960.

SMITH, MRS MARY E.C.

She was born in New York.
She moved to the south to teach religion. In 1890 she became Principal of Edward Waters College.

SMITH, JOHN HENRY

He was born in the city of Richmond, Virginia,U.S.A. He graduated from the Law School of Howard University in 1870. For eighteen years he was in the Civil Service. He became the U.S.A. Minister and Consul-General to Liberia.On retiring from the diplomatic service the Liberian President conferred upon him the order of Knight Commander of the Humane Order of African Redemption.

SISULU, WALTER

He was born in Transkei,South Africa, in 1912. For many years he was Secretary-General of the African National Congress. He was subjected to repeated bans, arrested and sentenced to life imprisonment on Robben Island.

SOBUKWE, ROBERT

He was born at Graaff in the Cape, South Africa, in 1924. He played a leading role in the founding of the Pan Africanist Congress, and in 1959 was elected its first President. He was sentenced to three year's imprisonment and released in 1963 but detained again on Robben Island by an Act of Parliament for six years.

SPRAGUE, MRS ROSETTA

She was born in New Bedford, Mass.,U.S.A., in 1839. She was the oldest child and the only living daughter of Frederick Douglas.
She married Nathan Sprague in 1863.

TALBERT, MRS MARRY B

She was born at Oberlin,Ohio,U.S.A. She graduated from Oberlin College, and accepted a position at Berthal University, Little Rock, Arkansas, in 1886. In 1887 she was elected Assistant Principal of the Little Rock High school, the highest position held by a woman in the State of Arkansas.

TERRELL, MRS MARY CHURCH

She was born in Memphis, Tenn.,U.S.A. In 1884 she graduated at Oberlin College. She was the first black woman who was appointed President of Bethel Literary and Historical Association in Washington, the foremost and oldest Lyceum established and controlled by black people in America. She served on the Board of education in the district of Columbia. In 1891 she married Robert H. Terrell who was appointed a judge by President Roosevelt.

TOIVO, HERMAN JA

He was born in 1925 in Namibia. He became regional secretary of SWAPO. He was arrested with 35 Namibians and deported to Pretoria, brought to trial under Terrorism Act and sentenced to 20 years imprisonment on Robben Island.

TOURE,SEKOU

He was born in 1922 in Guinea, West Africa. In 1945 he was appointed Secretary-General of the Post Office Workers Union. In 1958 Guinea became independent with him as its firts President. He was the founding member of the African Democratic Rally (R.D.A.) in 1946. He died in 1984.

TUBMAN, WILLIAM S.

He was born in 1895 in Liberia. He read Law and was called to the Bar in 1917. He became President of the Republic of Liberia in 1944.

TUCKER, PROF. THOMAS

He was born in Sierra Leone. He went to the U.S.A. to complete his education in 1856. He opened day and night schools for education of the newly freed race. President Grant advised him to accept the Liberian Mission but he rejected it.

TUHADELENI, ELISER

He was born in Namibia. He was a memeber of SWAPO Executive. He was acuused No.1 in the 1967-68 trial of 35 Namibians and sentenced to life imprisonment on Robben Island.

WASHINGTON, PROF. BOOKER T.

He was born in Franklin County, Virginia,U.S.A., in 1856. He attended Hampton Institute at Hampton, Virginia. Graduating in 1878, he was given a teaching position at the institute.
He was appointed the first principal of Tuskegee.His ambition was,"To give my life in providing as best I could the same kind of chance for self-help for the youth of my race".

WHITE, GEORGE H.

He was born in Bladen County,North Carolina. He entered Howard University, graduating in 1877. He later read Law and started his legal practice in 1879. He was elected to the North Carolina House of Representatives in 1889, and to the State Senate in 1884. He was later appointed prosecuting Attorney in 1886 and in 1896 was elected to the Congress. At the close of his second term in Congress he delivered a valedictory to the country,which was universaly praised as the best, truest and most timely expression of the Negro's plea for equality of citizenship that ever rang through the halls of Congress.

YATES, MRS JOSEPHINE SILONE

She was born in Mattiluck, Suffolk County,N.Y. She graduated from Rhode Island State Normal Collega in Providence. She taught science in Lincoln Institute, Jefferson City,Mo.
She was the first President of the Kansas City Women's League, National Association of Coloured Women.

YOUNG, WHITNEY

He was born in 1921,Lincoln Ridge,Kentucky. He was a social work administrator. He was appointed executive director of National Urban League, New York City, 1961-71. He was a member of the President's Commission on Law Enforcement and Administration of Justice.From 1954 to 1956 he was the Dean of the School of Social Work,Atlanta University. He died in 1971.

INDEX OF NAMES

INDEX CONTINUES

INDEX CONTINUES

END OF INDEX